The Relevance of Humanities to the 21st Century Workplace

The Relevance of Humanities to the 21st Century Workplace

Dr. Michael Edmondson

The Relevance of Humanities to the 21st Century Workplace

Copyright © Business Expert Press, LLC, 2020.

Cover image licensed by Ingram Image, StockPhotoSecrets.com

All rights reserved. No part of this publication may be reproduced, stored in a retrieval system, or transmitted in any form or by any means—electronic, mechanical, photocopy, recording, or any other except for brief quotations, not to exceed 400 words, without the prior permission of the publisher.

First published in 2020 by
Business Expert Press, LLC
222 East 46th Street, New York, NY 10017
www.businessexpertpress.com

ISBN-13: 978-1-95152-702-0 (paperback)
ISBN-13: 978-1-95152-703-7 (e-book)

Business Expert Press Human Resource Management and Organizational Behavior Collection

Collection ISSN: 1946-5637 (print)
Collection ISSN: 1946-5645 (electronic)

Cover and interior design by Exeter Premedia Services Private Ltd., Chennai, India

First edition: 2020

10 9 8 7 6 5 4 3 2 1

Printed in the United States of America.

For Lori, My humanities major for life

Abstract

The Relevance of the Humanities to the 21st Century Workplace provides a blueprint for higher education faculty, boards, presidents, senior leaders, parents, students, recent graduates, and other stakeholders. Blueprints are quintessential to any construction project. Also considered a set of vital communication tools, blueprints ensure that anyone involved in the project will understand what is required of the finished project. In the world of service organizations, blueprints can support innovation and diagnose problems in operational efficiency highlighting disconnects between what is offered and what people experience. Upon examining the state of humanities today, it becomes rather obvious that six disconnects exists. Colleges have done a poor job helping people outside the academy understand the terms liberal arts, humanities, liberal education, and liberal arts colleges (*The Explanation Disconnect).* Liberal arts and humanities faculty, as well as presidents, boards, and other stakeholders misunderstand the relevance of the humanities to the workplace (*The Comprehension Disconnect*). Higher education institutions need to improve how humanities majors translate their value to the marketplace (*The Translation Disconnect).* Administrators, faculty, and staff need to think differently and provide humanities majors with a modern perspective on career opportunities (*The Perception Disconnect).* In order for humanities majors to maintain relevance in the 21st century workplace, institutions need to teach students the dynamics involved with pursuing a vocation (*The Vocation Disconnect).* Finally, institutions need to help humanities majors increase their self-awareness in order for them to engage in self-determination and prepare for life after college accordingly (*The Cultivation Disconnect*). *The Relevance of the Humanities to the 21st Century Workplace* provides a blueprint that higher education administrators, faculty, and stakeholders can use in order to improve how people view, interact, and use the humanities in today's volatile, uncertain, complex, and ambiguous (VUCA) global marketplace. The challenges of automation, artificial intelligence, and yet to be invented technologies will continue to disrupt how people live, work, and learn. With colleges and universities slow to acknowledge the realities of today's issues, higher education leaders need to have a bias toward action and commit to explaining the relevance of the humanities to the 21st century workplace.

Keywords

higher education; humanities; liberal arts; career development; vocational guidance; college majors; academic programs; undergraduate education; personal development; professional development

Contents

Other Business Experts Press Books by Michael Edmondson xi
What People Are Saying About Edmondson's Other Books xiii
Foreword xxi
Preface xxiii
Introduction xxv

Chapter 1 The Explanation Disconnect 1
Chapter 2 The Comprehension Disconnect 21
Chapter 3 The Translation Disconnect 41
Chapter 4 The Perception Disconnect 61
Chapter 5 The Vocation Disconnect 83
Chapter 6 The Cultivation Disconnect 101

Conclusion 119
Recent Humanities Publications 127
About the Author 131
Index 133

Other Business Expert Press Books by Michael Edmondson

Strategic Thinking and Writing

Success Theory and Practice

Major in Happiness: Debunking the College Major Fallacies

Marketing Your Value: 9 Steps to Navigate Your Career

What People Are Saying About Edmondson's Other Books

In *Major in Happiness: Debunking the College Major Fallacies* Edmondson clearly debunks the myth that only certain college majors achieve greater success than others. More importantly, he maps a process to achieve and retain success and happiness which are two sides of a coin. A must read for parents and students thinking of going to college.

—Arun Tilak, Director—Center for Emerging Technology and Entrepreneurial Studies, Cameron University

In *Major in Happiness: Debunking the College Major Fallacies,* Edmondson's theories are accompanied by practical exercises that will be of value to students and their parents as they navigate a pathway through the complex interactions of study and work. He also points to two critical skills: team work and listening skills we expect and rarely teach. This book adds significantly to the debate about education and is a must read for incoming and exiting graduates and their parents.

—John Christian, President/CEO, CAPA, The Global Education Network

Major in Happiness: Debunking the College Major Fallacies is truly a thought-provoking book. This book certainly puts majors in perspective and the importance of doing what you love. This is a must read for parents of college bound students.

—Cindy Szadokierski, Executive Director, The Edge Program, Randolph-Macon College

Using strong research blended with a practical, clear writing style, Dr. Edmondson provides perspective and advice that the current generation of students (and parents) desperately needs to hear.

So many young people quickly abandon their passions and dreams to pursue majors and careers that they believe are "necessary" to achieve success and satisfaction in their vocational and personal lives. Edmondson pulls back the curtain on the misconceptions and fallacies that fuel that thinking, and outlines a compelling argument for the pursuit of a life driven by calling, purpose, and passion. As a professor in one of the disciplines that is often marginalized, I frequently work with students who are wrestling with the exact tensions that Edmondson describes, and I will certainly recommend *Major in Happiness: Debunking the College Major Fallacies* as a resource for those students in the future.

—Jeremy Osborn, PhD,
Associate Professor of Communication,
Cornerstone University

Major in Happiness: Debunking the College Major Fallacies presents an eye-opening presentation of the unique challenges of the 21st century college student. Edmondson offers more than just data to support his beliefs that perseverance, adaptability and life-long learning are keys to success. He provides an array of self-assessment tools to help students—and professionals alike—evaluate their unique value to corporations and the world. As a professor, this book has changed the way I will mentor my students. A must-read for all of us navigating through this quickly-changing landscape and trying to find *our* place in it.

—Laura Grayson Roselli, Professor,
Rowan College at Burlington County, and
Biopharmaceutical Consultant,
Kinetic Knowledge, LLC

Dr. Edmondson provides graduates and professionals with a road map to bring to practice Jonathan Winters' quote, 'If your ship doesn't come in, swim out to meet it.' Not only does he make a compelling case for swimming to meet the ship, he also provides readers with the knowledge of how to swim, and to swim in the right direction: the 'Assess, Brand, and Communicate' approach.

Marketing Your Value: 9 Steps to Navigate Your Career is an excellent read for college students, recent graduates and mid-career professionals as they navigate their careers and prepare for the next step towards their professional goals.

—Pareena Lawrence, PhD Provost and
Dean of the College Professor of
Economics Augustana College,
Rock Island, Illinois

Michael Edmondson brings many years of advising emerging undergraduates on the challenges and practical strategies for launching and adapting a career in a rapidly changing global economy. While giving substantial attention to self-marketing in a digital age, Edmondson's approach is founded self-evaluation—very much in the liberal-arts tradition—asking readers to assess their values and abilities in relation to opportunities and to regard the job search as a flexible, ever-changing process of self-exploration and assessment more than orientation to a fixed goal. In the tradition of *What Color is Your Parachute* and *What Should I Do With My Life?, Marketing Your Value: 9 Steps to Navigate Your Career* is likely to be invaluable to anyone who is entering the job market, considering a change of direction, or advising those who are.

—William Pannapacker, PhD Professor of English
Director of the Andrew W. Mellon Foundation
Scholars Program in the Arts and Humanities,
Faculty Director of the Great Lakes Colleges Association's
Digital Liberal Arts Initiative. Hope College

In *Marketing Your Value: 9 Steps to Navigate Your Career* Michael asks the tough and provoking questions that many of us struggle with on a day-to-day basis, such as understanding our personal mission, unveiling our distractions, and coming to terms with the major influence we have in our career development. This book provides an opportunity for professionals from any age, background, and industry the time to understand themselves through a series of thoughtful and challenging reflections and activities.

By doing this, Michael guides us back to our core to help us rediscover our values and use this knowledge as the foundation to successfully navigate a meaningful, and purposeful career.

—Yalitza M. Negron, M.S. Ed. Associate Director,
Office of Academic Community
Engagement Siena College

Marketing Your Value: 9 Steps to Navigate Your Career is an outstanding read and is applicable to any working individual's life. Dr. Edmondson's writing is clear, concise, and informative; a true reflection of the hardships many professionals, both young and old, face in today's highly competitive workforce. Through its various exercises and practices, Marketing Your Value will help anyone understand the tools, habits, and behaviors that are necessary when traveling the road to success. Dr. Edmondson has played an integral role in the launch of my career and continues to provide me with valuable insight along my professional journey. His immense knowledge on the topics of marketing and branding clearly shines through in this publication.

—Emily Nemeth Admissions Manager of
Ladywood High School (Livonia, MI)

Marketing Your Value is a practical resource filled with helpful tools and interesting anecdotes for assessing, branding, and communicating one's value—a valuable resource for anyone making a transition. I look forward to sharing it with my students.

—Steve VanderVeen, PhD Director of the Center for
Faithful Leadership at Hope College
Professor of Management.

Marketing Your Value: 9 Steps to Navigate Your Career is a practical book that illustrates how to successfully navigate career challenges in today's economy.

—Sheila Curran, President, Curran Consulting Group and
author of *Smart Moves for Liberal Arts Grads:
Finding a Path to Your Perfect Career*

Michael Edmondson has written the handbook for those striving to succeed in the new millennium. Instead of a run-of-the-mill self-help book, *Success Theory and Practice* connects the science, philosophy, and habits that drive individuals to success in today's marketplace. Success isn't a secret, and this book offers a roadmap for anyone willing to take on the challenge.

—Adam Cirucci Political consultant and journalist

Michael connects the dots in his book *Success: Theory and Practice* where the rubber meets the road with his 7 Characteristics of Success. He demonstrates the practical traits, backed up by fascinating research, to help you unfold your own success story.

—John P. Clark CFP® Financial Advisor and Retirement Living Expert

Michael Edmonson's *Success: Theory and Practice* is equal parts research and vision. This is how we do success in the 21st century: not only do we seek to improve our lot, but also our relationships, our self-awareness, and our world. Success is not either/or, but both/and.

—Evan Harris Co-owner of tapas yoga shala

Michael Edmonson's newest book *Success: Theory and Practice* is an absolute must read for both anyone entering the job market and those looking for growth in both their professional and personal lives. This book is not your everyday book on success, as it touches on the success of many, but lets you in on the mental and emotional challenges each faced throughout the journey. As quoted in the book from George Bernard Shaw "People are always blaming their circumstances for what they are. I do not believe in circumstances. The people who get on in this world are the people who get up and look for the circumstances that they want, and if they can't find them, make them." This book makes you want to find the circumstances you want in life.

—Rocco Marrari National Accounts Manager for EBE Technologies

Success: Theory and Practice is a must read for anyone who is interested achieving personal and professional success. Personal and professional growth is a key to success in our careers in this ever changing environment. Dr. Edmondson provides questions to ask ourselves periodically as a performance temperature check along with some quizzes. He also provides real life examples of successful individuals and traits they implemented to achieve their success.

—Robert Sauselein, CHST, HazTek, Inc.

Dr. Edmondson's writing style is clear and concise while including research relevant to theory and the practice of success. Choosing to read *Success: Theory and Practice* will challenge yourself to examine your own personal traits while receiving applicable advice on how to engage in successful behaviors, thus leading to personal and professional growth.

—Shelly Thomas Vroman, NP

Strategic Thinking and Writing is a must read for students and business professionals looking to enhance their strategic thinking and writing skills. Throughout the book, Dr. Edmondson provides readers the opportunity to perform thinking exercises and self-awareness checks which I found to be that are extremely helpful. Dr. Edmondson reminds us that writing is a process that we need to respect in order to produce a high-quality product.

—Monique Oudijk, Bayada Home Health Care

Thinking and writing well is one of the single most important traits you can have in the business world. Knowing how to think and write well helps you to perform and convey great ideas in your workplace. Dr. Edmondson's *Strategic Thinking and Writing* will help you capture your ideas and showcase them to your professional audience. Displaying great ideas with skill gives you power that is well deserved, and this book will help you achieve that easily.

—Katie Calabrese, National Association for Community College Entrepreneurship

In an era when more time is spent on constant tweeting than on critical thinking, Michael Edmondson provides an important reminder that the path to success won't be found by staying glued to a device. *Strategic Thinking and Writing* is a guide for effectively using the one key element needed to gain the upper hand in any challenging situation: your own thought process.

—Ronald Panarotti, Rider University

Dr. Edmondson's *Strategic Thinking and Writing* is a fascinating piece of literature that will help you remain focused, motivated, and engaged in the art of critical thinking. This book captures real life success stories and provides magnificent exercises, each designed to help people improve their strategic thinking and writing skills. This book has encouraged me to open up my mind, increase my self-awareness, and continuously strive for clear and efficient thinking.

—Martha Redondo, Princeton Theological Seminary

Foreword

Dr. Michael Edmondson continues his successful series of Business Expert books with a fresh look at the Humanities in *The Relevance of the Humanities in the 21st Century.* This book is an eye opener for the world of education and business to realize that the Humanities plays a major part in academia, business, and the ever changing world in which we live in.

As Michael states in *The Relevance of the Humanities in the 21st Century it* "provides a blueprint to help resolve the various disconnects that exist between higher education and the general public." Reading this book will help provide guidance to both parents and students on their academic journey, which at times appears confusing and disconnected. It also provides a blueprint for the business community to rethink their current impression that only a business degree is necessary for success.

My journey from Wall Street to the world of academia started after I had already achieved both a bachelor's and master's degree in Business. Tools to success were far between and most of the learning was based upon trial and error, thus having the tools available through Michael's book would have made my journey smoother and faster to the eventual senior position that I achieved. Then when I felt it was a time for "Plan B" during the volatile debt crisis era—I obtained my doctoral degree in business and transitioned over to higher education as a business professor. Again, having the tools to success would have also made it an easier transition. Then while I was the Chair of the Management Department I met a bright young man who had a vision—his name was Dr. Michael Edmondson.

Michael, to state a cliché, thinks "out of the box" and looks at everything from an alternative perspective. His advice on achieving success and the tools needed are clearly presented in this book, *The Relevance of the Humanities in the 21st Century.* He presents a new view and the relevance in today's society on an old topic—Humanities. As Michael states, "Senior executives who graduated with a humanities degree will routinely proclaim that their major taught them how to think critically, communicate clearly, analyze and solve complex problems, appreciate others, understand the physical world, and prepared them to learn continuously in order to work with others and on their own to meet the challenges of the future." Therefore, this small bit of advice pays large returns in the business community.

Michael has a very strong background in both business and academia—having been on the consulting side of business, the faculty side of academia, and now a Dean at a higher academic institution in New Jersey. His insights and first-hand knowledge of these topics are extremely helpful and relevant. His clear and concise views of the humanities is best summed up in a single sentence, as Michael stated: "This book provided an outline of strategies higher education institutions can use to help maintain the relevance of the humanities to the 21st century workplace." I trust you will enjoy this book as much as I have.

John Donnellan, DPS, MBA
Associate Professor and Chair, Management Department
NJCU School of Business

Preface

Prior to reading this publication, please become familiar with three definitions. First, the term *humanities* as used throughout this book refers to the following subjects: anthropology, art, dance, English, history, music, philosophy, political science, psychology or sociology. There are dozens more that could be included, but this abbreviated list provides the reader with the definitions needed to proceed. A more comprehensive list is found in Chapter 1. Second, the terms *humanities* and *liberal arts* are used interchangeably in this publication on purpose. Moreover, liberal arts colleges are not to be confused with the liberal arts subjects. While there are over 4,000 institutions of higher learning in the United States, just over 110 of them are classified as liberal arts colleges. This publication leaves the debate of defining a liberal arts college education to others. With that in mind, it is important to understand that one can receive a liberal arts education at thousands of colleges. Liberal arts colleges do not have the monopoly on teaching the humanities. Large four-year public research universities can, for example, have more history majors than those at a liberal arts school. Simply put, higher education has failed miserably in helping those outside of the academy understand the humanities and liberal arts. The debate on defining humanities versus the liberal arts has raged since the 1950s. This has to stop. Now. The near extinction of humanities on college campuses is a direct result of the inability of those in higher education to set aside their differences and solidify one common definition. *The Relevance of the Humanities in the 21st Century* provides a blueprint to help resolve the various disconnects that exist between higher education and the general public. The very survival of the humanities in today's volatile, uncertain, complex, and ambiguous (VUCA) global marketplace depends upon it.

Introduction

During the last few decades generally, and since the 2008 financial crisis specifically, the humanities discipline has been placed under tremendous scrutiny. "What are you going to do with that (fill in the blank—e.g., history) humanities degree?" is commonly asked at dinners, networking events, meetings, and other gatherings both on and off campuses of higher education institutions across the United States. Parents, students, board members, administrators, faculty, and just about every other stakeholder have all asked some form of that question. With a lack of a clear answer to that question, there is no surprise that the number of humanities majors has declined during the last decade. Two recent examples include the Modern Language Association (MLA) reporting that 651 foreign language programs have been closed recently and the American Historical Association (AHA) noting a 30 percent drop in history enrollments since the 2008 Great Recession.[1] As Brian C. Rosenberg, president of Macalester College, noted, "This wasn't a gradual decline; it was more like a tidal wave."[2]

Figure 0.1 summarizes why the number of humanities majors has declined during the last decade. Parents, students, and higher education stakeholders believe that professional degrees in business, nursing, and engineering will provide students with a clear career pathway to success. Success is often defined as declaring the perfect major, to land that perfect job that leads to that perfect life. This paradigm, however, often falls prey to that which no one has control over—reality. Today's students enroll in college for very practical reasons: to improve employment opportunities (91%); to make more money (90%); and to get a good job (89%).[3] Thus, the fundamental belief held by many is "if students do A (graduate from

[1] Laff, N. 2019. "Can Design Thinking Save the Humanities?" *LinkedIn*, April 3.

[2] Kirsch, A. 2019. "Stop Worrying About the 'Death' of the Humanities." *The Wall Street Journal*, April 26, https://wsj.com/articles/stop-worrying-about-the-death-of-the-humanities-11556290279?ns=prod/accounts-wsj

[3] Craig, R. 2017. "The Top 10 Higher Education Issues We All Agree On." *Forbes*, January 20. (accessed February 21, 2019).

Figure 0.1 Success

college) they should get B (jobs and money)." The path to success should resemble the left line in the image: a linear trajectory to wealth, professional attainment, and career achievements.

The fact that business majors now account for about one out of every five bachelor's degrees and the number of majors in almost every humanities field has declined since 2008 demonstrates the preference for a linear career path.[4] As Fareed Zakaria wrote, "This dismissal of broad-based learning, however, comes from a fundamental misreading of the facts and puts America on a dangerously narrow path for the future."[5] The problem with this mental model is that the path to success for most resembles the right line in the image. Nonlinear career pathways, serendipity, and

---

[4] Benjamin, S. 2018. "The Humanities Are in Crisis," *The Atlantic*, August 23.

[5] Zakaria, F. 2015. "Why America's Obsession with STEM Education is Dangerous." *The Washington Post*, March 26. https://washingtonpost.com/opinions/why-stem-wont-make-us-successful/2015/03/26/5f4604f2-d2a5-11e4-ab77-9646eea6a4c7_story.html?noredirect=on&utm_term=.1f4643352959 (accessed November 5, 2018)

being able to adapt to market conditions are more often the hallmarks of a professional navigating today's ever-changing global marketplace. This dichotomy between desire—a linear career path—versus reality—a non-linear trajectory—succinctly summarizes the reasons behind the continual decline of the humanities.

This dichotomy exists because of numerous factors such as the rising cost of education coupled with a diminishing field of well-paying employment opportunities, allowing graduates to repay their student loans. As *Forbes* noted,

> One of the primary issues facing higher education is the rising cost of education balanced against the benefit of a college degree. As valuable as a college education is, the cost is often the first and most important factor people face in weighing the value of universities.[6]

Since "many recent graduates are underemployed and face massive student loan debt," people want a guaranteed career path that provides a high-paying salary with benefits.[7] This desire for a return on investment (ROI) is compounded by outdated assumptions about college students, namely that most are 18- to 22-year-olds fresh out of high school. According to the Lumina Foundation, "that's no longer the reality as 38% of college students today are older than 25, and 58% work while in college (about 40% of community-college students and 20% of four-year students work 20+ hours per week). Another 26% are raising kids."[8] It's no wonder then that college students are demanding an ROI.

---

6 Allaire, J. 2018. "Five Issues Facing Higher Education in 2018." *Forbes*, January 15. https://cornerstone.edu/blogs/lifelong-learning-matters/post/five-issues-facing-higher-education-in-2018 (accessed April 2, 2018).

7 Allaire, J. 2018. "Five Issues Facing Higher Education in 2018." *Forbes*, January 15, 2018. https://cornerstone.edu/blogs/lifelong-learning-matters/post/five-issues-facing-higher-education-in-2018 (accessed April 2, 2018).

8 Lumina Foundation. "Our assumptions About College Students are Wrong." undated and published at https://luminafoundation.org/todays-student (accessed February 21, 2019).

With the sole focus of securing employment after graduation, this current mental model needs to be viewed as a powerful determinant of choices and behaviors, an automated algorithm if you will, dictating how students have responded to global events.[9] The irony in the current mental model, so many college students use is that the career prospects of humanities majors has never been greater.[10] Bard College president Leon Botstein noted in a May 24, 2019, interview published in *The Wall Street Journal* that "Liberal arts graduates do extremely well, compete very successfully in a rapidly changing world. They acquire the skills of improvisation, of learning, of adaptation, of articulating who they are and what they want."[11] Three such examples are history majors who become well-paid lawyers or judges after completing law degrees, philosophy majors who leverage their analytical and argumentative skills on Wall Street and international-relations majors who thrive as overseas executives for large corporations.[12] Research has demonstrated that chief executives leverage their liberal arts and humanities education throughout their entire career.

For example, one 2008 survey of 652 U.S.-born chief executives and heads of product engineering at 502 technology companies found that 92 percent held bachelor's degrees divided among three categories of academic majors: 37 percent held an engineering or computer technology degree, 33 percent majored in business or finance, and the remaining 30 percent graduated with a liberal arts or humanities degree.[13] Senior executives who graduated with a humanities degree will routinely proclaim that their major taught them how to "think critically, communicate clearly,

---

[9] Chan, K.W., and R. Maugorgne. March 2015. "Red Ocean Traps." *Harvard Business Review*.

[10] Benjamin, S. 2018. "The Humanities Are in Crisis." *The Atlantic*, August 23.

[11] Akst, D. 2019. "The Reopening of the Liberal Mind." *The Wall Street Journal*, May 24. https://wsj.com/articles/the-reopening-of-the-liberal-mind-11558732547?ns=prod/accounts-wsj (accessed May 25, 2019).

[12] Anders, G. 2017. "The Unexpected Value of the Liberal Arts." *The Atlantic*, August 1. https://theatlantic.com/education/archive/2017/08/the-unexpected-value-of-the-liberal-arts/535482/ (accessed January 21, 2019).

[13] Vivek, W., F. Richard, and R. Ben. 2008. *Education and Tech Entrepreneurship*, May 1,. Available at SSRN: https://ssrn.com/abstract=1127248 or http://dx.doi.org/10.2139/ssrn.1127248

analyze and solve complex problems, appreciate others, understand the physical world, and prepared them to learn continuously in order to work with others and on their own to meet the challenges of the future."[14] Humanities majors and graduates need to understand that the demand for their skills set continues to remain both relevant and lucrative within the 21st century workplace. As Mark Schneider and Matthew Sigelman noted in *Saving the Liberal Arts*, "by the time liberal arts majors with advanced degrees reach the 'peak earning ages,' 56–60, they earn on average $2,000 more per year than those with advanced professional degrees in law or medicine."[15]

Since the 2008 financial crisis, however, higher education institutions have struggled to address this dichotomy while trying to find answers to other issues such as declining state revenue, managing tuition costs, increasing student retention and graduation rates, recruiting from a shrinking pool of 18-year-olds, developing online programs to reach new students, and maintaining campuses with grounds and building that require constant upkeep. As a demonstration of how financially unhealthy higher education is in the United States both Moody's and Fitch ratings issued a negative outlook for the sector for 2019. Fitch director Emily Wadhwani noted that lower-tier institutions are especially vulnerable and "could suffer disproportionately from near-term constraints on tuition growth, price sensitivity, longer term demographic shifts, and increasing uncertainty on federal and state regulatory and funding support."[16] For those institutions struggling financially, options include consolidating programs, restricting course offerings, hiring freezes, furloughing staff, transitioning some faculty from tenure track to adjunct positions, and

---

[14] Strauss, V. 2015. "What the 'Liberal' in 'Liberal Arts' Actually Means." *The Washington Post*, April 2. https://washingtonpost.com/news/answer-sheet/wp/2015/04/02/what-the-liberal-in-liberal-arts-actually-means/?noredirect=on&utm_term=.ef65a6da69e7 Accessed December 10, 2018.

[15] Schneider, M., and M. Sigelman. February 2018. *Saving the Liberal Arts: Making the Bachelor's Degree a Better Path to Labor Market Success*. American Enterprise Institute.

[16] Fitch Ratings press release dated December 6, 2018, "Fitch Ratings Revises U.S. Higher Education Sector Outlook to Negative for 2019." https://fitchratings.com/site/pr/10054235 (accessed December 10, 2018).

reducing campus services that students rely on such as mental-health services or library hours.[17] In a growing number of cases, consolidation of campuses through mergers, acquisitions, or affiliations is a necessity. So too are closures. More than 100 for-profit and career colleges closed between the 2016–17 and 2017–18 academic years alone, while 20 non-profit colleges shuttered during that period, according to data from the National Center for Education Statistics.[18] Future outlooks continue to remain bleak as evidenced by Clayton Christensen who suggested that 50 percent of U.S. colleges and universities will close or go bankrupt during 2014 to 2024.[19] Subhash Kak echoed similar sentiment and observed that "unless universities move quickly to transform themselves into educational institutions for a technology-assisted future, they risk becoming obsolete."[20] Amid a dynamic, hypercompetitive, and ever-changing landscape marked by continuous technological disruption, thousands of institutions are seeking ways to adapt. This adaptation will play a critical role in helping the humanities remain relevant to the 21st century workplace.

As higher education institutions look to create, implement, and assess new strategic initiatives in order to remain competitive, they first need to recognize that, for the most part, they have failed at three tasks related to the humanities. First, colleges have failed at helping those outside of the academy understand the term humanities as well as their relevance to the 21st century workplace. Second, institutions have fallen far short in helping students translate their humanities education and undergraduate experience for future employers. Finally, universities need to vastly

---

[17] Harris, A. 2018. "The Liberal Arts May Not Survive the 21st Century." *The Atlantic*, December 13. (accessed December 28, 2018).

[18] Arnett, A.A. 2018. "More than 100 for-Profit Institutions Closed During Past Year, According to Federal Data." *Education Drive*, June 6. https://educationdive.com/news/more-than-100-for-profit-institutions-closed-during-past-year-according-to/525094/ (accessed July 10, 2018).

[19] Horn, M. 2018. "Will Half of All Colleges Really Close in the Next Decade?" *Forbes*, December 13. https://forbes.com/sites/michaelhorn/2018/12/13/will-half-of-all-colleges-really-close-in-the-next-decade/#5cbf73cf52e5 (accessed December 22, 2018).

[20] Kak, S. 2018. "Will Traditional Colleges and Universities Become Obsolete,?" *The Smithsonian*, January 10. (accessed February 21, 2019).

improve the guiding principles of their career preparation for students and alumni. Launching and navigating a career in today's volatile, uncertain, complex, and ambiguous (VUCA) global marketplace demands that higher education institutions implement a sophisticated, savvy, and dynamic plan to help students achieve and sustain professional success.

The retail market can attest to just how disruptive today's market is. In February 2019, American discount footwear retailer Payless ShoeSource announced it was closing all of it 2,100 stores throughout the United States. A few months later in May, the discount clothing manufacturer Dress Barn announced it was closing all of its 650 U.S. stores. "According to data from Coresight Research, American retailers have announced plans to close 5,994 stores in 2019. That's 140 more than were announced in all of 2018, but short of the more than 8,000 announced in 2017."[21] One observer noted,

> The pace of disruption in retail is widely acknowledged. Yet, the pace of change inside retailers continues to lag. Many retailers find themselves trapped in a cycle of continuing to chase consumer trends. Without bold action, the retail landscape will continue to be scattered with bankruptcies.[22]

A similar observation can be made for higher education. The pace of disruption in higher education is widely acknowledged. Yet, the pace of change inside higher education continues to lag. Many colleges and universities find themselves trapped in a cycle of continuing to chase consumer trends. "Higher education will need to adapt if they want to survive."[23] Without bold action, innovative thinking, or creative problem-solving,

---

[21] Taylor, D.B. 2019. "Dressbarn Closing All 650 Stores." *The New York Times*, May 21. https://nytimes.com/2019/05/21/business/dressbarn-closing.html?login=email&auth=login-email (accessed May 22, 2019).

[22] Garcia, A. 2019. "Payless is Closing All Its 2,100 US Stores." *CNN*, February 18. https://cnn.com/2019/02/15/business/payless-closing-stores-bankrupt/index.html (accessed February 20, 2019).

[23] Pringle, B. 2018. "Parents Increasingly Refuse to Pay for College." *Washington Examiner*, September 4. https://washingtonexaminer.com/red-alert-politics/parents-increasingly-refuse-to-pay-for-college (accessed February 24, 2019).

the higher education landscape will continue to be scattered with mergers, acquisitions, and closures. And the humanities will become irrelevant to the 21st century workplace.

But implementing creative problem-solving is often met with resistance within higher education. As Kate Ebner and Noah Pickus observed, "innovation is about seeing new possibilities in old problems. To do this, academic leaders must have a clear-eyed view of the issues and a willingness to define the challenge creatively."[24] Identifying the issues, defining the challenges, and proposing solutions are all invitations to personal and professional growth for higher education administrators "if they are willing to grow."[25] But from the vantage point of many, it appears that such willingness remains a distant dream. Cathy N. Davidson declared that "Our educational systems, so far, look as if the Internet hasn't been invented yet. Scratch most conventional academic departments and you see little hint of restructured courses, let alone restructure thinking."[26] The continued belief held by higher education officials that they are doing an excellent job prohibits the realization required to present new solutions in order to maintain relevance.

In the first episode of the HBO television series *The Newsroom*, Jeff Daniels plays the news anchor Will McAvoy who sits on a panel on a university campus. A college student stands up and asks the panel to answer the question, "What makes the United States the greatest country in the world?" In his response, McAvoy leverages both logic and emotion to illustrate that the United States, despite the perception held by many, is not the greatest country in the world anymore. McAvoy goes on to state that "the first step in solving any problem is recognizing there is one." Higher education leaders need to recognize the disconnections that exist in order to illustrate the relevance of the humanities to the 21st century

---

[24] Ebner, K., and N. Pickus. 2018. "The Right Kind of Innovation." *Inside Higher Ed*, July 25. https://insidehighered.com/digital-learning/views/2018/07/25/yes-higher-ed-needs-innovation-it-should-be-right-kind-opinion (accessed February 24, 2019).

[25] Ebner, K., and N. Pickus. 2018. "The Right Kind of Innovation." *Inside Higher Ed*, July 25. https://insidehighered.com/digital-learning/views/2018/07/25/yes-higher-ed-needs-innovation-it-should-be-right-kind-opinion (accessed February 24, 2019).

[26] Davidson, C.N. 2011. "So Last Century." *The Times Higher Education*, April 28.

workplace. A 2014 Gallup-Lumina Foundation study found that while 96 percent of chief academic officers of colleges and universities believe that their institutions are "very or somewhat effective" at preparing students for the workforce, only 11 percent of business leaders "strongly agree."[27] Leaders of higher education institutions have a huge disconnect between the results of their efforts and the end product via graduates as assessed by business leaders. Colleges and universities can ill afford to be out of touch with the needs of employers. Administrators and faculty need to recognize the needs of the business community and develop programs to address them. Doing so would demonstrate to students that their tuition would result in a return on their investment.

Writing in *Forbes*, Ryan Craig noted,

> Unless and until colleges and universities are able to document that liberal arts programs actually produce the outcomes we've taken on faith, this exodus will continue and liberal arts programs will be increasingly a plaything for rich kids (who'll use connections to get good first jobs, so it doesn't matter what they study).[28]

Craig went on to suggest that institutions need to do a far better job of providing assessments that point to the necessity of critical thinking, problem-solving, and situational judgment to potential employers as a way to convince people of the value of the humanities to the 21st century workplace. As Purdue president Mitch Daniels has said, "higher education has to get past the 'take our word for it' era. Increasingly, people aren't."[29] Now, more than ever, college and university administrators need

---

[27] Rusiloski, B. 2017. "Solving the Vast Disconnect Between Schools and Employers." *Technically Philly*, October 6. https://technical.ly/philly/2017/10/06/solving-disconnect-schools-employers/ (accessed January 11, 2019).

[28] Craig, R. 2017."The Top 10 Higher Education Issues We All Agree On." *Forbes*, January 20. https://forbes.com/sites/ryancraig/2017/01/20/the-top-10-higher-education-issues-we-all-agree-on/#763a4f39fa87 (accessed February 21, 2019).

[29] Craig, R. 2015. "We've Reached Peak College." *Forbes*, November 5. https://forbes.com/sites/ryancraig/2015/11/05/weve-reached-peak-college/#63120abc2b22 (accessed February 21, 2019).

to talk with employers.[30] Lynn Pasquerella, president of the Association of American Colleges and Universities (AAC&U), stated, "it's critical for colleges to show they're taking the public's concern about their value seriously, and giving graduates the capacity to deal with a future that none of us can fully predict."[31]

The Relevance of the Humanities to the 21st Century Workplace provides a blueprint for higher education to faculty, boards, presidents, senior leaders, parents, students, recent graduates, and other stakeholders. Blueprints are quintessential to any construction project. Also considered a set of vital communication tools, blueprints ensure that anyone involved in the project will understand what is required of the finished project. In the world of service organizations, blueprints can support innovation and diagnose problems in operational efficiency, highlighting disconnects between what is offered and what people experience. Upon examining the state of humanities today, it becomes rather obvious that six disconnects exist. *The Relevance of the Humanities to the 21st Century Workplace* provides a blueprint that higher education administrators, faculty, and stakeholders can use in order to improve how people view, interact, and use the humanities in today's VUCA global marketplace.

The Six Disconnects

- *Chapter 1—The Explanation Disconnect*: Colleges have done a poor job helping people outside the academy understand the terms liberal arts, humanities, liberal education, and liberal arts colleges. To address this explanation disconnect, institutions can help individuals outside of higher education clearly understand the humanities by implementing four strategies. First, schools need to clearly define the terms liberal, arts, and

---

[30] Rusiloski, B. 2017. "Solving the Vast Disconnect Between Schools and Employers." *Technically Philly*, October 6. https://technical.ly/philly/2017/10/06/solving-disconnect-schools-employers/ (accessed January 11, 2019).

[31] Supiano, B. 2018. "Colleges Say They Prepare Students for a Career, Not Just a first Job. Is That True?" *The Chronical of Higher Education*, August 28.

education. Second, institutions need to communicate what subjects are included in the definition of the humanities. Third, schools must explain the difference between a liberal arts college and a liberal arts education. Finally, colleges and universities must provide a clear and compelling explanation of the terms liberal arts and a liberal education. These four strategies form the foundation for helping people understand the relevance of the humanities to the 21st century workplace.

- *Chapter 2—The Comprehension Disconnect:* Liberal arts and humanities faculty, as well as presidents, boards, and other stakeholders, misunderstand the relevance of the humanities to the workplace. To address this comprehension disconnect, institutions can help individuals outside of higher education clearly understand the value of humanities majors to the workplace by implementing various strategies. First, schools need to tell the compelling stories of CEOs and other senior executives that graduate with a humanities major. Second, institutions must explain how there is no one specific business pedigree that individuals need to get to the corner office. Finally, colleges and universities must illustrate to students that employers value skills and credentials far more than they do one's academic major.
- *Chapter 3—The Translation Disconnect:* Higher education institutions need to do a far better job helping humanities majors, as well as majors in other subjects, translate their value to the marketplace. To address this translation disconnect, colleges and universities can help humanities majors translate their value to the marketplace via a clear, concise, and compelling story by implementing four strategies. First, colleges need to help students uncover the one word that would serve as the focus of their personal story. Second, institutions should teach humanities majors how to develop their value proposition—a statement in less than seven words that illustrates their current position in the marketplace. Third, schools should assist humanities majors in defining their success factors so they can place them at the top of their resume

and use them in interviews. Finally, colleges and universities need to provide opportunities for humanities majors to craft a personal statement that summarizes how their skills, knowledge, and experiences are relevant to the workplace.

- *Chapter 4—The Perception Disconnect:* Administrators, faculty, and staff need to think differently and provide humanities majors with a different perspective on different career opportunities. To address this perception disconnect, higher education institutions can help humanities majors expand their career horizons by implementing three strategies. First, colleges need to illustrate to humanities majors that they have three career paths available to them: knowledge, issue, and skill. Second, institutions should teach humanities majors about the wide spectrum of employment opportunities outside of the academy. Finally, faculty need to have an honest conversation about graduate school with those students interested in applying.
- *Chapter 5—The Vocation Disconnect:* In order for humanities majors to maintain relevance in the 21st century workplace, institutions need to implement three specific strategies that will improve how faculty explain the various factors involved with launching a career and pursuing a vocation. First, institutions need to provide internship or apprenticeship opportunities for humanities majors. Second, colleges should incorporate the study of grit into their curriculum so humanities majors can understand this vital element involved with long-term career success. Finally, faculty should include discussions of recent evidence illustrating the different winding career paths available to college graduates.
- *Chapter 6—The Cultivation Disconnect:* Institutions need to help humanities majors increase their self-awareness in order for them to engage in self-determination and prepare for life after college accordingly. To address this cultivation disconnect, higher education institutions can help students increase their self-awareness in today's VUCA global marketplace by implementing five strategies. First, colleges need to introduce,

> and then explain, the five areas of well-being as students make the transition from campus to career. Second, institutions must incorporate more discussions of the relationship between self-awareness, self-discipline, and the development of one's self. Third, schools have an obligation to create programming that allows students to engage in self-determination. Fourth, colleges and universities need to include the theory and practice of positive uncertainty as part of the student experience. Finally, higher education institutions must provide lifelong learning opportunities for their alumni.

The challenges of automation, artificial intelligence, and yet to be invented technologies will continue to disrupt how people live, work, and learn. With colleges and universities slow to acknowledge the realities of today's issues, higher education leaders need to have a bias toward action and commit to explaining the relevance of the humanities to the 21st century workplace.[32]

---

[32] Kak, S. 2018. "Will Traditional Colleges and Universities Become Obsolete?" *The Smithsonian*, January 10. https://smithsonianmag.com/innovation/will-traditional-colleges-universities-become-obsolete-180967788/ (accessed February 21, 2019).

CHAPTER 1

The Explanation Disconnect

> Fortune does favor the bold and you'll never know what you're capable of if you don't try.
>
> —Sheryl Sandberg, *Lean In: Women, Work, and the Will to Lead*

Introduction

The first disconnect concerns the words liberal arts, humanities, liberal arts colleges, and liberal education. Over the last few decades, higher education administrators, faculty, and board members have failed at explaining those outside of the academy understand those words. The end result has been constant confusion over the definition of each word as well as the relevance of a humanities education in a volatile, uncertain, complex, and ambiguous (VUCA) global marketplace. In a world of constant disruption, change, and hyperconnectivity, higher education can ill afford to have this understanding disconnect. As Cass Cliatt from Brown University noted, "We know we have a problem with the term (liberal arts). The problem is in our own communities. We've spent so much time defending the term that we're not talking about we're doing."[1] During a January 2019 conference, Howard Gardner from Harvard University presented information from a long-term study where his team interviewed more

---

[1] Ben, U. 2019. "4 Lessons on Liberal Education's Future." *Education Drive*, January 28, https://educationdive.com/news/4-lessons-on-liberal-educations-future/546981/?utm_source=Sailthru&utm_medium=email&utm_campaign=Issue:%202019-01-28%20Higher%20Ed%20Education%20Dive%20Newsletter%20%5Bissue:19140%5D&utm_term=Education%20Dive:%20Higher%20Edhttps://www.nytimes.com (accessed February 15, 2019)

than 2,000 students, faculty members, trustees, parents, alumni, and others affiliated with 10 institutions of different types. His earlier conclusion from the data is that the phrase "liberal arts and sciences" isn't widely understood. Many respondents couldn't define the liberal arts at all or defined it incorrectly.[2] Additionally, "many people don't understand what a liberal education actually is."[3] To address the explanation disconnect, this chapter explains the extent of it and then provides a blueprint on how each college can address it moving forward. Detailing the explanation disconnect involves understanding the confusion surrounding the terms liberal arts, humanities, liberal arts colleges, and liberal education. Only then can a conversation begin surrounding the relevance of the humanities to the 21st century workplace.

Explaining the Disconnect

The first step in explaining the liberal arts is recognition that the term itself causes so much confusion that even its more ardent supporters fail to fully recognize what the term means. In 1970, author Wayne C. Booth noted this dilemma and wrote that since the defenders of liberal education are growing more confused with each passing year, there could come a day when "there are no true defenders left."[4] Although his premonition has yet to become a reality what is very true today is the severe confusion surrounding the term liberal arts. According to Ernest Pascarella in *What We Don't Know about the Effects of Liberal Arts Education*, "the definition of liberal arts is problematic."[5] If the defenders of liberal arts are chal-

---

[2] Rick, S. 2019. "Small Colleges Grapple with 'Culture of Insecurity." *Inside Higher Ed*, January 8, https://insidehighered.com/news/2019/01/08/private-college-presidents-seek-adapt-changing-market (accessed February 24, 2019).

[3] Valerie, S. 2015. "What the 'Liberal' in 'Liberal Arts' Actually Means." *The Washington Post*, April 2. https://washingtonpost.com/news/answer-sheet/wp/2015/04/02/what-the-liberal-in-liberal-arts-actually-means/?noredirect=on&utm_term=.ef65a6da69e7 (accessed December 10, 2018).

[4] Wayne, C.B. 1970. *Now Don't Try To Reason With Me: Essays And Ironies For A Credulous Age*, 201. Chicago: University of Chicago Press.

[5] Quote found in Blaich, Charles, Anne Bost, Ed Chan, and Richard Lynch. 2004. "Defining Liberal Arts Education." Center of Inquiry in the Liberal Arts.

lenged by a problematic definition, then the first step toward a deeper understanding of liberal arts should involve an examination of the extent of this confusion.[6] In Justin Stover's "Case for the Humanities" published in *The Chronicle of Higher Education*, he admitted that "the humanities are not just dying—they are almost dead...and have become a loosely defined collection of technical disciplines." He then declared that "the result of this is deep conceptual confusion about what the humanities are and the reason for studying them in the first place." With a level of hubris so commonly found among higher education boards, administrators, and faculty. Stover concluded by writing "most of us know the humanities when we see them." No, they do not. Herein lies the explanation disconnect.[7]

Simply put, the confusion about the liberal arts involves everyone from the high-school student and parent to the undergraduate faculty, staff, and administration. This confusion has lasted centuries and continues into the 21st century. The College of Idaho's 2010-11 Catalog stated this very succinctly: "Liberal arts is a frequently misunderstood phrase."[8] "Too often those involved in liberal arts education, faculty, staff and administrators, as well as students have only a fairly vague sense of its meaning, and those meanings are often in conflict with one another."[9] In 2006, Ronald A. Williams, president of Prince George's Community College, said that defining liberal arts education is "particularly problematic"

---

[6] I should point out that confusion surrounding other academic programs is also very common. For example, "the majority of Americans are not clear about what engineers do" according to Grasso, D. November 2002. *Engineering a Liberal Education*. University of Vermont Publication.

[7] By Justin, S. 2018. "Case for the Humanities." *The Chronicle of Higher Education,* March 04. https://chronicle.com/article/There-Is-No-Case-for-the/242724 (accessed May 25, 2019).

[8] The College of Idaho 2010-2011 Catalog located at http://collegeofidaho.edu/media/catalog/Liberal_Arts.asp

[9] Christian, W.H. No Date. "Liberal Arts Traditions and Christian Higher Education: A Brief Guide." Institute for Liberal Arts at Westmont College, http://westmont.edu/institute/pdfs/liberal_arts_tradition.pdf

and that "the need to figure out just what a liberal education is" remains a critical issue that should be addressed.[10]

Whether it's enrolling at a liberal arts college, selecting a liberal arts major, or classifying their higher education institution, the evidence suggests that faculty, staff, and administration, as well as students and parents, are all unable to consistently define a liberal arts education. "According to Charles Wegener, the term is so overloaded with meanings that 'it is a good question whether it should be retained.'"[11] Since it continues to be retained across all levels of education, however, administrators need to ensure that students and parents, as well as their entire faculty and staff, have a clear, consistent, and compelling definition of what liberal arts education is in the 21st century. Doing so can help an "institution consider its unique value that it adds to a world in which information is everywhere."[12] And since "many parents cannot help but notice that after a while, most colleges and universities start to look alike" identifying and explaining a school's unique value is critical to its future.[13]

Researcher Scott Jaschik noted this lack of understanding regarding the liberal arts during his walk around Dartmouth's campus when he "found that even those students who say they value liberal education don't necessarily know what it is."[14] When Jaschik asked students to explain what liberal arts education means "two answers came up again and again: the classes are small and the professors really care about their students and reach out to them."[15] In 2005 the Association of American Colleges and

---

[10] "Promoting Liberal Education." Inside Higher Education, January 30, 2006.

[11] Daniel, M. 2008. *The Educated Person: Toward A New Paradigm For Liberal Education,* 1. Lanham, Maryland: Rowman & Littlefield Publishers, Inc.

[12] *2010 Horizon Report,* p. 3. The 2010 Horizon Report is a collaboration between The New Media Consortium and the Educause Learning Initiative An Educause Program. To download a copy of the report visit http://wp.nmc.org/horizon2010/

[13] Paul, B. 2003. *College* Rankings Exposed: The Art Of Getting A Quality Education In The 21st Century, 28. Lawrenceville, NJ: Peterson's.

[14] Scott, J. 2004. "How to Talk About Liberal Education (If You Must)." Boston.com, November 21.

[15] Scott, J. 2004. "How to Talk About Liberal Education (If You Must)." Boston.com, November 21.

Universities (AAC&U) conducted focus groups to explore how students viewed and defined liberal education. The research confirmed that "most of the high school and college students had not heard the term liberal education and were unable to provide an accurate definition."[16] As one Portland high school student said,

> I associate it [liberal education] with a broad education and openness to different things. It's an education that will prepare me for what I need to know either at the present time in my life or for my future. It's a good point that you take what you can from it.[17]

These findings were echoed by John Strassburger, former president of Ursinus College, who participated in market research focus groups with representatives from several other schools. The focus groups involved parents of high school students who just completed the college search process and sought to discover what people thought about liberal education and liberal arts colleges. According to Strassburger, "The results were not pretty as 19 of the 20 parents had definitions of 'liberal arts' that no educator would even recognize."[18] The parents "agreed that liberal arts referred to either studying soft, touchy feely subjects, like psychology as opposed to physics, or studying something leftish that came out of the 60s."[19] Strassburger's counterpart at Washington & Jefferson College, Tori Haring-Smith, also realized this confusion and said, "I don't think many high school students really know what liberal arts is and we need to do a better job of explaining because the term is confusing to some people."[20]

---

[16] Debra, H., and A. Davenport. Summer/Fall 2005. "What Really Matters in College: How Students View and Value Liberal Education." Liberal Education.
[17] Debra, H., and A. Davenport. Summer/Fall 2005. "What Really Matters in College: How Students View and Value Liberal Education." Liberal Education.
[18] Strassburger, J. 2010. "For the Liberal Arts, Rhetoric Is Not Enough." *The Chronicle of Higher Education*, February 28.
[19] Strassburger, J. 2010. "For the Liberal Arts, Rhetoric Is Not Enough." *The Chronicle of Higher Education*, February 28.
[20] Sam, A. 2008. "Liberal Arts Degrees Misunderstood by Many." *Pittsburgh Post-Gazette*, October 14.

In *The University in a Corporate Culture*, Eric Gould bluntly summarized the situation and wrote: "The public simply does not know [the definition of liberal arts]; and the academy does not make the meaning clear."[21] Gould also examines the results of a 1997 survey conducted for Richard Hersh, president of Hobart and William Smith Colleges, that concluded only 14 percent of high school students and only 27 percent of parents claimed to be very familiar with liberal arts education. Noting the extent of the confusion within and outside of the academy, only 32 percent of university and specialty school graduates and 54 percent of business executives claimed familiarity with the term liberal education.[22]

> It's no wonder there is so much confusion about the phrases liberal arts and liberal education. In addition, the use of the word sciences appears in the phrase arts and sciences! Different variations of these phrases can be found throughout today's discussions: the liberal arts, the liberal arts and sciences, liberal education, liberal arts education, and liberal arts and sciences education. Each time one is used it has the potential to mean different things to different people.[23]

In one of the great ironies in this movement to expand liberal arts in Singapore, one observer noted while there have been high levels of enthusiasm for the creation of liberal arts schools, "there appears to be fundamental misunderstanding of what a liberal arts college is and can

---

[21] Eric, G. 2003. *The University in a Corporate Culture,* 13, New Haven: Yale University Press.

[22] Eric, G. 2003. *The University in a Corporate Culture,* 13, New Haven: Yale University Press.

[23] Valerie, S. 2015. "What the 'Liberal' in 'Liberal Arts' Actually Means." *The Washington Post,* April 2. https://washingtonpost.com/news/answer-sheet/wp/2015/04/02/what-the-liberal-in-liberal-arts-actually-means/?noredirect=on&utm_term=.ef65a6da69e7 (accessed December 10, 2018).

offer. Additionally, the idea of a liberal arts college appears to be misunderstood, even by proponents of the scheme."[24]

To address this explanation disconnect, institutions can help individuals outside of higher education clearly understand the humanities by implementing four strategies. First, schools need to clearly define the terms liberal, arts, and education. Second, institutions need to communicate what subjects are included in the definition of the humanities. Third, schools must explain the difference between liberal arts college and liberal arts education. Finally, colleges and universities must provide a clear and compelling explanation of the terms liberal arts and a liberal education. These four strategies form the foundation for helping people understand the relevance of the humanities to the 21st century workplace.

Etymology

The word *liberal* derives from the Latin *liberalis,* meaning "of freedom; worthy of a free man, gentlemanlike, courteous or generous."[25] According to William Cronon, Frederick Jackson Turner and Vilas Research Professor of History, Geography, and Environmental Studies at the University of Wisconsin-Madison, the word liberal "actually has much deeper roots, being akin to the Old English word *leodan,* meaning 'to grow,' and *leod,* meaning 'people.'"[26] In his article "Only Connect...the Goals of a Liberal Education," Cronon further explained that liberal "is also related to the Greek word *eleutheros,* meaning 'free,' and goes all the way back to the Sanskrit word *rodhati,* meaning 'one climbs' or 'one grows.'"[27]

The second word *arts* is also derived from a variety of languages. It is often explained as having its origins from the Latin *artes* meaning "skill,

---

[24] 2007. "Clarifying the Liberal Arts Education in Singapore." *Singapore Angel,* December 27.

[25] Latin Dictionary and Grammar Aid. *University of Notre Dame,* found online at http://archives.nd.edu/cgi-bin/lookup.pl?stem=liberalis&ending

[26] Cronon, W. Autumn 1998. "'Only Connect...' The Goals of a Liberal Education." *The American Scholar* 67, no. 4, pp. 73–80.

[27] Cronon, W. Autumn 1998. "'Only Connect...' The Goals of a Liberal Education." *The American Scholar* 67, no. 4, pp. 73–80.

method or technique."[28] It can also trace its roots to the Old French *artem* meaning "art, skill or craft" and from the Greek *arti* meaning "just" or *artios* meaning "complete." Thus, when combined, the term *liberal arts* are classically defined as the "studies pursued by free men and women."[29] During this time, *free* referred to a "citizen with rights and economically independent, as a member of a wealthy leisure class. In other words, 'liberal arts' originally meant something like 'skills of the citizen elite' or 'skills of the ruling class.'"[30] By tracing the etymology of both words, we have discovered what they were but not why someone would study the liberal arts. For that understanding, we turn our attention to the etymology of the word education.

Authors Robert Nola and Gürol Irzik defined the etymology of education as stemming from the Latin *educare*, to bring up, rear, or foster especially in relation to children and *educere*, meaning to lead.[31] Martha W. Gilliland, chancellor of the University of Missouri-Kansas City, in a speech on the occasion of the Sesquicentennial Celebration of Catawba College, went further and said that "*education* comes from the Latin *educare* meaning 'to lead out of the darkness.' To lead a learner to new understandings...to journey to a new plane of experience....to shine a light on dark corners of ignorance."[32] When the etymology of education is added to this classic definition of the words liberal and arts, we can conclude that liberal arts education consists of studies pursued by free men and women in order to shine a light on dark corners of ignorance and learn new understandings.

In the words of Pamela Schwandt, "The liberal arts are those studies which set the student free from prejudice and misplaced loyalties and free

---

[28] *Online Etymology Dictionary* located at http://etymonline.com/

[29] Shoenberg, R. Winter 2009. "How Not to Defend Liberal Arts Colleges." *Liberal Education* 95, no. 1, pp. 56–59.

[30] Lind, M. 2006. "Why the Liberal Arts Still Matter." *Wilson Quarterly*, September 22.

[31] Nola, R., and G. Irzik. 2005. Philosophy, Science, Education and Culture, 4. Springer: The Netherlands.

[32] Martha, W.G., Chancellor, University of Missouri-Kansas City. December 3, 2001 "The Liberal Arts: To Lead out of the Darkness, To Equip Citizens for Success in the Circumstances of Their Times." Speech on the Occasion of the Sesquicentennial Celebration of Catawba College.

for service, wise decision making, community leadership, and responsible living."[33] Kathleen Haney agreed and further explained that

> The liberal arts are the arts of using language. If one were to master the liberal arts, then one would master human nature. Here is where the *libre* of liberal comes in—such a person would thereby be freed from the ancient enemies which plague humankind—the liberal arts are the liberating arts that free humankind from its worst enemies, ignorance and prejudice.[34]

Exactly what subjects are included within the scope of liberal arts education that avail themselves to students in order to "shine light on dark corners of ignorance" in order to "free humankind from its worst enemies" is the focus of the next section.

List of Subjects

The original definition of the subjects included in the liberal arts was based on classical antiquity. The original liberal arts subjects provided a practical education that developed mental capacity, designed in the late medieval period (12th and 13th centuries), and used ideas from Ancient Greek and Roman cultures. The seven liberal arts were taught in two groups: the *trivium* and the *quadrivium*.[35]

The *trivium* (Latin for three ways) included the literary disciplines:

- *Grammar*, the science of the correct usage of language. It helps a person to speak and write correctly.
- *Dialectic* (or logic), the science of correct thinking. It helps you to arrive at the truth.

---

[33] Pamela, S, ed. No Date. "Called to Serve: St. Olaf and the Vocation of a Church College." Located at http://gustavus.edu/faith/pdf/called_to_serve.pdf

[34] Kathleen, H. August 10–15, 1998. "The Liberal." *Arts and the End of Education.* Twentieth World Congress of Philosophy. Boston, Massachusetts.

[35] https://simple.wikipedia.org/wiki/Liberal_arts#The_seven_liberal_arts

- *Rhetoric*, the science of expression, especially persuasion. Ways of organizing a speech or document. Adapting it so that people understand it and believe it.

The *quadrivium* (Latin for four ways) included the disciplines connected with mathematics. They were:

- *Arithmetic* teaches about numbers;
- *Geometry* teaches about calculating spaces;
- *Astronomy* teaches about the stars;
- *Music* teaches ratio and proportion and is related to melody and song as it was in the Middle Ages.

When examining the number of subjects included within the definition of liberal arts today, however, it is important to remember that "the number of subjects liberal arts encompasses has multiplied" over the centuries and continues to grow.[36] In short, the modern definition of liberal arts or humanities includes, but is not limited to, the following list of subjects:

•Ancient languages
•Anthropology
•Art
•Astronomy
•Biology
•Chemistry
•Classics
•Comparative literature
•East Asian studies
•Economics
•English
•Foreign languages
•Geography
•Geology
•History
•International studies
•Mathematics
•Modern languages
•Music
•Philosophy
•Religion
•Rhetoric

Selecting one of the aforementioned academic subjects does not, however, necessarily mean a student receives a liberal education. This in and of itself is problematic and still confuses many faculty, staff, and

[36] 2010. "In Praise of the Liberal Arts." Speech presented by Princeton University President Shirley M. Tilghman at the Lawrenceville School, April 6.

administrators of higher education institutions as well as others and deserves a brief examination.

Liberal Arts Versus Liberal Education

There is a critical difference between a liberal arts education and a liberal education. Understanding the distinction between the two provides a solid foundation for addressing the other types of confusion surrounding the liberal arts. In 2009 Robert Shoenberg, senior fellow at the Association of American Colleges and Universities (AAC&U), published an article "How Not to Defend Liberal Arts Colleges" and highlighted a distinction between the two and noted that the terms liberal arts education and liberal education "are not synonymous."[37] *Liberal arts* refers to certain disciplines (such as history, philosophy, or English to name just a few), "which may be pursued to many possible ends" while *liberal education* "may be pursued through *any subject matter* (emphasis added) but the term implies distinct purposes: breadth of awareness and appreciation, clarity and precision of thought and communication, critical analysis, and the honing of moral and ethical sensibilities."[38]

To further clarify the difference between a liberal arts education and a liberal education, Shoenberg stated "an education in the liberal arts and sciences disciplines is not, by definition, a liberal education. Study exclusively in the liberal arts disciplines does not guarantee a liberal education."[39] Liberal arts majors in history, philosophy, or English, for example, can be trained in as narrow a specialized field as any professional program such as engineering, medicine or teaching. Conversely, many career-specific programs are insistent on liberal learning."[40]

---

[37] Shoenberg, R. Winter 2009. "How Not to Defend Liberal Arts Colleges." *Liberal Education* 95, no. 1, pp. 56–59.

[38] Shoenberg, R. Winter 2009. "How Not to Defend Liberal Arts Colleges." *Liberal Education* 95, no. 1, pp. 56–59.

[39] Shoenberg, R. Winter 2009. "How Not to Defend Liberal Arts Colleges." *Liberal Education* 95, no. 1, pp. 56–59.

[40] Shoenberg, R. Winter 2009. "How Not to Defend Liberal Arts Colleges." *Liberal Education* 95, no. 1, pp. 56–59.

The 2010 American Society for Engineering Education (ASEE) conference that had a special interest group devoted to liberal education serves as an example of Shoenberg's two contentions that a liberal education may be pursued through any subject matter and that some career-specific programs are insistent on liberal learning. According to attendee Robert Talbert, Associate Professor of Mathematics and Computing Science at Franklin College, participants agreed that liberal education "integrates multiple perspectives into understanding what engineers study and do and believe in teaching metacognitive skills and preparing students to be human beings, not just workers."[41] In his article, "Engineering and A Liberal Education," Domenico Grasso echoed this integration of engineering with a liberal education and wrote: "The social sciences and humanities must assume parity with mathematics and the sciences in the preparation of well-educated engineers. Society can ill afford engineers with a casual exposure to social sciences and the humanities."[42] Integrating the study of engineering with a liberal education allows for students to gain a deeper understanding required of the intersection between technology and human nature in order to achieve a sustainable and equitable utilization of resources and global security.[43]

The Association of American Colleges and Universities offers a more complete definition of liberal education and defines it as learning "that empowers individuals and prepares them to deal with complexity, diversity, and change. It provides students with broad knowledge of the wider world (e.g., science, culture, and society) as well as in-depth study in a specific area of interest."[44] Thus, liberal education provides students with a much needed sense of social responsibility, a transferable set of practical skills such as communication, analytical and problem-solving,

---

[41] Talbert, R. 2010. "What (Some) Engineers Think About Liberal Education." *Blog Entry*, June 21. http://castingoutnines.wordpress.com/2010/06/21/what-some-engineers-think-about-liberal-education/

[42] Grasso, D. November 2002. *Engineering a Liberal Education*. University of Vermont Publication.

[43] Grasso, D. November 2002. *Engineering a Liberal Education*. University of Vermont Publication.

[44] "What is Liberal Education." Association of American Colleges and Universities. Definition found at http://aacu.org/leap/what_is_liberal_education.cfm

and a demonstrated ability to apply knowledge and skills in real-world settings.[45] Researcher Vivek Wadhwa observed:

> The key to good design is a combination of empathy and knowledge of the arts and humanities. Musicians and artists inherently have the greatest sense of creativity. You can teach artists how to use software and graphics tools; turning engineers into artists is hard. Creating solutions such as these requires a knowledge of fields such as biology, education, health sciences and human behavior. Tackling today's biggest social and technological challenges requires the ability to think critically about their human context, which is something that humanities graduates happen to be best trained to do.[46]

Scholars such as Martha Nussbaum, Francis Horn, Andrew Chrucky, and Leo Strauss offer similar views on liberal education. In a speech at Carleton College, Nussbaum noted that

> an education is truly liberal only if it is one that liberates the student's mind, encouraging him or her to take charge of his or her own thinking, leading the Socratic examined life and becoming a reflective critic of traditional practices. [47]

In "Education among the Liberal Arts," Horn echoed a similar sentiment and defined "the outcome of a liberal education as a harmonious development of the physical, moral and intellectual qualities of each

---

[45] "What is Liberal Education." Association of American Colleges and Universities. Definition found at http://aacu.org/leap/what_is_liberal_education.cfm

[46] Wadhwa, V. 2018. "Why Liberal Arts and the Humanities are as Important as Engineering." *The Washington Post,* June 12. https://washingtonpost.com/news/innovations/wp/2018/06/12/why-liberal-arts-and-the-humanities-are-as-important-as-engineering/?noredirect=on&utm_term=.128ec50ffca9 (accessed December 12, 2018).

[47] Martin Nussbaum, M. 2002., "Liberal Education and Global Responsibility.," A Talk for a Symposium at Carleton College, in Honor of the Inauguration of Robert A. Oden, Jr. as President, October 25, 2002.

individual."[48] While examining the definitions of liberal education as put forth by three scholars, all of which argued that liberal education involved an amoral component, Chrucky disagreed and argued that liberal education is one that "encompasses cognitive, moral, and emotional education."[49] For Strauss, "liberal education is training in the highest form of modesty and demands from us the complete break with the noise, the thoughtlessness and the cheapness of the Vanity Fair of the intellectuals as well as of their enemies."[50] As president emeritus of both the University of Iowa and Dartmouth College, James O. Freedman remarked that "liberal education urges upon us a reflectiveness, a carefulness to be open to correction and new insight that can mitigate these tendencies toward polarity, rigidity, and intolerance."[51]

In addition to scholars, schools have also developed their own definitions of liberal education. The Harvard University defines liberal education as

> the kind of learning that heightens students' awareness of the human and natural worlds they inhabit. It makes them more reflective about their beliefs and choices, more self-conscious and critical of their presuppositions and motivations and more able to inform themselves about the issues that arise in their lives, personally, professionally and socially.[52]

Swarthmore College offers a similar definition and classifies liberal education as one that has "consistently helped students learn to question

---

[48] Horn, F.H. November 1951. "Education Among the Liberal Arts." *Journal of Higher Education* 22, no. 8, pp. 411–457.

[49] Chrucky, A. 2003. "The Aim of a Liberal Education." September 1, and posted at http://ditext.com/chrucky/aim.html

[50] Strauss, L. 1959. "What Is Liberal Education?" Address Delivered at the tenth Annual Graduation Exercises of the Basic Program of Liberal Education for Adults (accessed June 6, 1959).

[51] Freedman, J.O. *Liberal Education & the Public Interest,* 56. Iowa City: University of Iowa Press.

[52] 2007. "Report on the Task." Force on General Education, 8. Harvard University, Faculty of Arts and Sciences.

and explore, to think critically, to develop their imaginations, and to act responsibly and with conviction."[53]

Liberal Education and Political Liberalism

Two recent developments have compounded the confusion surrounding the terms liberal arts education and liberal education. The first misconception concerns the term liberal education and modern liberal thinking as it relates to the political environment in the United States. To the untrained observer, liberal arts might well produce liberal thinkers. Only individuals who employ a false etymology, however, associate the liberal arts with political liberalism.[54] Political liberalism is completely different from a liberal arts education or a liberal education.

The president of the National Humanities Center, W.R. Connor, noted this difference and stated: "When we say liberal education, we are not, of course talking about the dreaded 'L' word of recent American political sloganeering, nor are we even referring to the free play of ideas as in traditional liberal political theory."[55] Cronon also believed that "In speaking of 'liberal' education, we certainly do not mean an education that indoctrinates students in the values of political liberalism."[56] Political liberalism forms a specific paradigm associated with governance while a liberal arts education refers to the articulation of a specific curriculum that has evolved over two millennia.

The second issue that needs clarification concerns the ideological preference of college and university professors. If a professor teaches at a liberal arts school or designs a curriculum based on liberal education, that does not necessarily make modern American political liberalism their ideological preference. Labeling all liberal arts professors as liberals falls far short

---

[53] Introduction to *The Meaning of Swarthmore*, collection of essays by Swarthmore alumni, published at http://swarthmore.edu/news/meaning/

[54] Lind, M. 2006. "Why the Liberal Arts Still Matter." *Wilson Quarterly*, September 22.

[55] Connor, W.R. No Date. "Liberal Arts Education in the Twenty-First Century." American Academy for Liberal Education, Keynote Remarks, Kenan Center Quality Assurance Conference. Chapel Hill, North Carolina.

[56] Cronon, W. 1998 "'Only Connect…' The Goals of a Liberal Education." *The American Scholar* 67, no. 4, pp. 73–80.

in adequately describing the group dynamics of any particular department or school. As Jere P. Surber wrote in the *Chronicle of Higher Education*,

> It doesn't make sense to speak of the political persuasions of the academy as a whole. Anyone who has been to a faculty meeting lately, at an institution of any size, knows that faculty members from business schools are typically the most conservative, followed, in order, by the natural sciences, the social sciences, and liberals in the liberal arts.[57]

To account for the nuances and dynamics of individuals, departments, and schools, Surber also observed that "not every liberal-arts professor is politically liberal, nor is every business instructor politically conservative." [58] Further evidence of this diversity along the political spectrum is found in Michael Bérubé's book *What's LIBERAL about the Liberal Arts?* where he cites Higher Education Research Institute data on political attitudes.

> In a survey covering 55,521 faculty in 416 institutions from 1989 to 2001-02 the data illustrated that the number of liberals among faculty grew from 42 percent to 48 percent while the centrists shrank from 40 percent to 34 percent and conservatives held steady at 18 percent.[59]

---

[57] Surber, J.P. 2010. "Well Naturally We're Liberal." *Chronicle of Higher Education*, February 7. Also see Laster, J. 2010. "College Makes Students More Liberal, but Not Smarter About Civics." *The Chronicle of Higher Education,* February 5.

[58] Surber, J.P. 2010. "Well Naturally We're Liberal." Chronicle of Higher Education, February 7. Also see Cohen, P. 2010. "Professor is a Label That Leans to the Left." *Chronicle of Higher Education*, January 18.

[59] Quote found in National Academic Advising Association (NACADA) presentation by E. Timothy Moore MFA, Liberal Arts Advising Commission Chair, no date provided. Also see Bérubé, M. 2006. *What's Liberal About the Liberal Arts?: Classroom Politics and "Bias" in Higher Education*. W. W. Norton & Company, and Wolfe, A. 2006. "Defending the PhDs." *New York Times,* September 10.

Liberal Arts Colleges and Liberal Arts

The last aspect of the understanding disconnect that requires explanation remains a brief discussion surrounding the term liberal arts college and the type of education offered at one. The three most common characteristics of a liberal arts college are small student populations, no graduate programs, and mainly residential in nature. But not all institutions with a small student body are liberal arts colleges. Many people, including faculty and staff at higher education institutions, fail to understand if their school is officially classified as liberal arts school. As former Utica College president Todd Hutton stated,

> Part of the confusion is also the result of students and parents thinking of Utica College as a liberal arts college, based solely on the fact that it is a small, private college. This confusion, which is even shared by some of Utica's faculty and staff, is not uncommon in the world of higher education.[60]

If the faculty of an institution are confused, it should come as no surprise that those outside of the academy are as well. Each institution has a responsibility to identify, explain, and then communicate its classification in clear, concise, and compelling manner for anyone to understand. In additional to the classification of an institution, the other component of this understanding disconnect concerns the type of education offered at a liberal arts college.

Jonathan Veitch, president of Occidental College in California, described liberal arts college education when he stated "a liberal arts college takes seriously the notion that a job isn't a job, it's a vocation, so it better bring meaning to your life and help you think through what that might look like."[61] Maud S. Mandel, president of Williams College in

---

[60] Hutton, T.S. 2006. "The Conflation of Liberal & Professional Education: Pipedream, Aspiration, or Nascent Reality?" *Liberal Education.*

[61] Moody, J. 2018. "What a Liberal Arts College Is and What You Should Know." *U.S. News and World Report,* December 7. https://usnews.com/education/best-colleges/articles/2018-12-07/what-a-liberal-arts-college-is-and-what-students-should-know (accessed March 3, 2019).

Massachusetts, echoes that sentiment as she considers a liberal arts education to be "an introduction to general knowledge, or even the scope of human knowledge as we know it so far," while allowing students to explore interests and curiosities through experiential education opportunities such as study abroad trips, internships, and community service.[62] But this emphasis on general knowledge and allowing students to explore interests and curiosities is common in many mission statements of public universities around the United States. In short, liberal arts colleges do not have a monopoly on providing students with a liberal education or a liberal arts education. Students at public universities and those attending a liberal arts college can both study the humanities. Moreover, public universities with tens of thousands of students, graduate programs, and large commuter populations also offer a liberal education curriculum, experiential education opportunities, and a general education curriculum grounded in the humanities. The size and diversity of the student body, the programs of study, the physical location of the campus, the net tuition cost of an undergraduate degree, and the graduation rate form the key characteristics separating institutions of higher learning in the United States.

Conclusion

To help the humanities maintain their relevance the understanding disconnect involving liberal arts, humanities, liberal arts colleges, and liberal education needs to be resolved. Higher education administrators, faculty, and board members have to do a much better job educating the general public around a commonly agreed upon definition for each word. Leaders from every type of college and university need to standardize these terms so that the general public can have a better understanding of higher education. Colleges and universities can ill afford to leave this understanding disconnect unresolved. Increased regulation, falling enrollment,

[62] Moody, J. 2018. "What a Liberal Arts College Is and What You Should Know." *U.S. News and World Report*, December 7. https://usnews.com/education/best-colleges/articles/2018-12-07/what-a-liberal-arts-college-is-and-what-students-should-know (accessed March 3, 2019).

and skyrocketing tuition costs are all characteristics of the U.S. higher education industry. This may be particularly difficult for those working at liberal arts colleges struggling to maintain enrollment. Efforts such as the website liberalartscolleges.com actually create more confusion, not less. This website, and others like it, inadvertently suggest that only liberal arts colleges can provide a liberal education and that is simply untrue. Such marketing tactics, when coupled with the explanation disconnect, only compound the problems for institutions trying to remain open in today's volatile, uncertain, complex, and ambiguous (VUCA) global marketplace. More than 100 for-profit and career colleges across the United States closed between the 2016–17 and 2017–18 academic years alone, while 20 nonprofit colleges shuttered during that period, according to data from the National Center for Education Statistics,

> That consolidation also had an impact on the priorities of ones that remained open. Institutions are adding degree programs in emerging tech fields such as artificial intelligence, dropping low-enrollment programs including some in the liberal arts, and looking online where they can reach a bigger audience with niche subject matter.[63]

If the humanities are to remain pertinent to the 21st century workplace, higher education leaders, faculty, and board members will need to do a far better job of explaining how the liberal arts have always been relevant in the first place.

---

[63] Busta, H. 2019. "How Many Colleges and Universities have Closed Since 2016?" *Education Drive*, March 9, https://educationdive.com/news/how-many-colleges-and-universities-have-closed-since-2016/539379/ (accessed March 21, 2019).

CHAPTER 2

The Comprehension Disconnect

> Happiness does not come from a job. It comes from knowing what you truly value, and behaving in a way that's consistent with those beliefs.[1]
>
> —Mike Rowe

Introduction

Employers understand the value of the humanities. They did decades ago and continue to do so. Unfortunately, many higher education leaders and faculty have failed to understand, communicate, and educate students on this view expressed by employers. When higher education institutions recognize the value employers place on the humanities, students and graduates will have a better sense of how to apply their liberal arts education to employment opportunities. Unfortunately, since the post–World War II era of the 1950s and continuing until the present day, college graduates have, often with little help from those inside higher education, learned how to apply their humanities major to the workplace. Learning how to apply their humanities education to real-world situations benefited those with an entrepreneurial mindset. One such example is Starbucks CEO Howard Schultz. In his 1999 business memoir, *Pour Your Heart Into It*, Schultz recalled: "To my parents, I had attained the big prize: a diploma. But I had no direction. No one ever helped me see the value

---

[1] Quote found at http://lifebuzz.com/mike-rowe/ (accessed May 2, 2019).

in the knowledge I was gaining."[2] And why do many administrators, faculty, and staff fail to help students understand how employers value the humanities? The research suggests that those inside higher education believe they are doing an excellent job; so why change? The research also indicates, however, that those outside of higher education, the employers hiring college graduates, believe otherwise. Therein lies the catalyst driving this understanding disconnect. If the humanities are to remain relevant to the 21st century workplace, the understanding disconnect must be understood and addressed.

Explaining the Understanding Disconnect

In 2012, the HBO launched a new series called *The Newsroom*. In the first episode, Jeff Daniels plays news anchor Will McAvoy who sits on a panel at a university campus discussion regarding the current state of American politics. In addition to Daniels' character McAvoy, there are two other panelists and a moderator. The lecture hall is filled to capacity with college students. Toward the end of the conversation, a college student stands up and asks the panel to answer the question, "What makes the United States the greatest country in the world?" In his response, McAvoy leverages both logic and emotion to illustrate that the United States, despite the perception held by many, is not the greatest country in the world anymore. McAvoy goes on to state that "the first step in solving any problem is recognizing there is one." Board, presidents, senior executives, and faculty at colleges and universities across the United States need to recognize the problem. A 2014 Gallup-Lumina Foundation study found that while 96 percent of chief academic officers of colleges and universities believe that their institutions are "very or somewhat effective" at preparing students for the workforce, only 11 percent of business leaders "strongly agree."[3]

---

[2] Linshi, J. 2015. "10 CEOs Who Prove Your Liberal Arts Degree Isn't Worthless." *Time*, July 25. http://time.com/3964415/ceo-degree-liberal-arts/ (accessed February 22, 2019).

[3] Rusiloski, B. 2017. "Solving the Vast Disconnect Between Schools and Employers." *Technical.ly Philly*, October 6, https://technical.ly/philly/2017/10/06/solving-disconnect-schools-employers/ (accessed January 11, 2019).

Leaders of higher education institutions have a huge disconnect between the results of their efforts and the end product via graduates as assessed by business leaders. In today's volatile, uncertain, complex, and ambiguous (VUCA) global marketplace, administrators, and faculty can ill afford to be out of touch with the needs of employers. Administrators and faculty need to recognize the needs of the business community and develop programs to address them. One specific program consist of helping undergraduates understand how to apply their humanities education to the 21ast century workplace. Doing so would demonstrate to students how they could purposefully create a return on their investment. Writing in *Forbes*, Ryan Craig noted,

> Unless and until colleges and universities are able to document that liberal arts programs actually produce the outcomes we've taken on faith, this exodus will continue and liberal arts programs will be increasingly a plaything for rich kids (who'll use connections to get good first jobs, so it doesn't matter what they study).[4]

Craig went on to suggest that institutions need to be a far better job of providing assessments that point to the necessity of critical thinking, problem-solving and situational judgment to potential employers as a way to convince people of the value of the humanities to the 21st century workplace.

As Purdue president Mitch Daniels has said, "higher education has to get past the 'take our word for it' era. Increasingly, people aren't."[5] Now, more than ever, college and university administrators need to talk with employers.[6] For decades, employers have valued graduates

---

[4] Craig, R. 2017. "The Top 10 Higher Education Issues We All Agree On." *Forbes*, January 20. https://forbes.com/sites/ryancraig/2017/01/20/the-top-10-higher-education-issues-we-all-agree-on/#763a4f39fa87 (accessed February 21, 2019).

[5] Craig, R. 2019. "We've Reached Peak College." *Forbes*, November 5. https://forbes.com/sites/ryancraig/2015/11/05/weve-reached-peak-college/#63120abc2b22 (accessed February 21, 2019).

[6] Rusiloski, B. 2017. "Solving the Vast Disconnect Between Schools and Employers." *Technical.ly Philly*, October 6. https://technical.ly/philly/2017/10/06/solving-disconnect-schools-employers/ (accessed January 11, 2019).

from the humanities. In one industry after another, across all types of employment positions, and throughout the country, employers have proven time and again that they will hire humanities majors for a wide variety of jobs outside of the narrow scope often discussed on college campuses. Until greater discussions evolve, the understanding disconnect will continue. Lynn Pasquerella, president of the Association of American Colleges and Universities (AAC&U), stated "it's critical for colleges to show they're taking the public's concern about their value seriously, and giving graduates the capacity to deal with a future that none of us can fully predict."[7] With such a competitive market for students, however, admission officers and marketing departments tend to give students what they want instead of what is necessary for them to success postgraduation.

> Colleges and universities are pandering to the students and giving them what they want, instead of what the employers want. I don't think you have to make a distinction between getting skills and getting an education. We need to do both.[8]

Unfortunately, evidence suggests that "there is a stark misalignment between the talents employers demand and the skills graduates have as they enter the U.S. workforce. And many higher education leaders fail to see it."[9] If higher education institutions are to demonstrate the relevance of the humanities to the 21st century workplace, they first have to recognize their problem. In a VUCA global marketplace marked by continual disruption, higher education institutions have failed to demonstrate the relevance of the humanities to the 21st century work-

---

[7] Supiano, B. 2018. "Colleges Say They Prepare Students for a Career, Not Just a first Job. Is That True?" *The Chronical of Higher Education*, August 28. https://chronicle.com/article/Colleges-Say-They-Prepare/244376 (accessed September 10, 2018).

[8] Johnson, L. 2011. "Employers Say College Graduates Lack Job Skills." *The Chronicle of Higher Education*, December 5.

[9] Francis, J., and Z. Auter. 2017–2018. "3 ways to Realign Higher Education With Today's Workforce." Center for Education and Workforce, June 20.

place. That is a problem and higher education boards, administrators, faculty, and other stake holders need to recognize that the disconnect exists.

Approximately 60 percent of executives and hiring managers think that most college graduates are prepared to succeed in entry-level positions.[10] But only a third of executives, and a quarter of hiring managers, believe graduates have the skills and knowledge to advance or be promoted. The majority of business executives and hiring managers believe that colleges need to make improvements to ensure that graduates gain the skills and knowledge needed for success.[11]

Employers value a four-year college degree, many of them more than ever. Yet half of those surveyed by *The Chronicle of Higher Education* and American Public Media's *Marketplace* said they had trouble finding recent graduates qualified to fill positions at their company or organization. Nearly one-third gave colleges just fair to poor marks for producing successful employees.[12] And they dinged bachelor's degree holders for lacking basic workplace proficiencies, like adaptability, communication skills, and the ability to solve complex problems. "Woefully unprepared" is how David E. Boyes characterized the newly minted B.A.'s who apply to his Northern Virginia technology consulting company.[13] "The mismatch between what students are interested in and what employers are willing to pay for may be the biggest impediment to a rewarding career for the newest generation of American workers."[14]

---

[10] Supiano, B. 2018. "Colleges Say They Prepare Students for a Career, Not Just a first Job. Is That True?" *The Chronical of Higher Education*, August 28.

[11] 2018. "Fulfilling the American Dream: Liberal Education and the Future of Work." *Association of American Colleges and Universities*, https://aacu.org/research/2018-future-of-work-presentation (accessed February 2, 2019).

[12] Fischer, K. 2013. "The Employment Mismatch." *The Chronicle of Higher Education*, March 4. https://chronicle.com/article/The-Employment-Mismatch/137625?cid=rclink (accessed December 7, 2018).

[13] Fischer, K. 2013. "The Employment Mismatch." *The Chronicle of Higher Education*, March 4. https://chronicle.com/article/The-Employment-Mismatch/137625?cid=rclink (accessed December 7, 2018).

[14] Newman, R. 2012. "Where the Jobs Are, the College Grads Aren't." *U.S. News and World Report*, May 14.

Liberal arts and humanities faculty, as well as presidents, boards, and other stakeholders have failed to help people outside of the academy comprehend the relevance of the humanities to the workplace. To address this comprehension disconnect, institutions can help individuals outside of higher education clearly understand the value of humanities majors to the workplace by implementing four strategies. First, schools need to tell the compelling stories of CEOs and other senior executives that graduate with a humanities major. Second, institutions must explain how there is no one specific business pedigree that individuals need to get to the corner office. Finally, colleges and universities must illustrate to students that employers value skills and credentials far more than they do one's academic major.

CEOs Who Were Liberal Arts Majors

During the last 20 years, executives from different industries have either graduated with a humanities degree or publicly endorsed the value of one. Priceline CEO Jeff Boyd attributes much of his success to his liberal arts background. His humanities education allowed him to "have a broad understanding not just of how businesses work but how people work."[15] Like many executives Boyd maintained an interest in hiring people with the right skill set and personality who would fit into the organizational culture. When considering a recent college graduate as a new employee Boyd considers the candidate's "intellect, energy and the ability to get things done" over college attended, grade point average, or major.[16] Senior executives like Boyd have demonstrated a consistent capacity to hire job candidates with a humanities degree because many leaders have similar backgrounds themselves, know that there is no one path to the corner office, and have identified the essential skills to long-term career success. Higher education officials and faculty would serve themselves and the humanities well by leveraging these three strategies to address the understanding disconnect.

---

[15] No Date. "CEOs with Liberal Arts Degrees Running the Fortune 1000." Liberal Arts Colleges.

[16] No Date. "CEOs with Liberal Arts Degrees Running the Fortune 1000." Liberal Arts Colleges.

Faculty, staff, and administrators across colleges and universities need to help students understand the CEOs who graduated with a humanities degree. Students need to understand that humanities majors can have a successful career trajectory and obtain the corner office if that is indeed what they seek. Business majors do not have the monopoly on getting to the corner office. David M. Rubenstein, the cofounder of the Carlyle Group, believes the focus on science, technology, engineering, and mathematics at the expense of literature, philosophy and other areas in the humanities has cost American students critical thinking and problem-solving skills that enable them to achieve success in the business world. Career-specific skills can be learned later, he said, noting that many of Wall Street's top executives studied the humanities.[17] The following list represents just a small sample size of the many CEOs and senior executives who graduated with a humanities degree. Since the mental model currently employed by so many college students focuses on declaring a major in business in order to find a job upon graduation, the list only contains those who achieved a senior position in business. The list excludes individuals who graduated with a humanities degree and who succeeded in fields outside of business such as musicians, actors, and athletes. The list is arranged by alphabetical order by last name.

- *Jill Barad, an English major from Queens College, New York City:* She began her career in cosmetics sales, while still attending Queens College in New York. After graduating with a Bachelor of Arts degree in English Literature and Psychology, she became brand manager for the full line of Coty products. This was followed by a move to Los Angeles and the position of account executive for the Max Factor brand at Wells, Rich, Greene/West advertising agency. In 1981, she started at Mattel, Inc. as a product manager. In 1997 she was named Mattel's chief executive officer (CEO) and chairman of the Board.

[17] Bray, C. 2014. "Carlyle Co-Founder's Formula for Success: Study the Humanities." *The New York Times*, January 23. https://dealbook.nytimes.com/2014/01/23/carlyle-co-founders-formula-for-success-study-the-humanities/ (accessed February 17, 2017).

- *Carol Browner, an English major from University of Florida*: She is an American lawyer, environmentalist, and businesswoman, who served as director of the White House Office of Energy and Climate Change Policy in the Obama administration from 2009 to 2011. Browner previously served as the administrator of the Environmental Protection Agency (EPA) during the Clinton administration from 1993 to 2001. She currently works as a senior counselor at Albright Stonebridge Group, a global business strategy firm.
- *Ely Callaway, History major from Emory University*: He had three successful careers—first in textiles, next in wine and finally in golf. "Most people would settle for any one of Callaway's careers," *Entrepreneur* magazine wrote of Ely Callaway in a 1994 profile.
- *Kenneth Chenault, History major from Bowdoin College*: He is an American business executive. He was the CEO and chairman of American Express from 2001 until 2018. He is the third African American CEO of a Fortune 500 company.
- *Tim Donahue, English major from John Carroll University*: He would go on to hold a variety of executive positions in the telecommunications industry. *Forbes Magazine* rated Mr. Donahue as one of America's leading chief executive officers with an approval rating of 87 percent.[18]
- *Donna Dubinsky, History major from Yale University:* She is an American business leader who played an integral role in the development of personal digital assistants (PDAs) serving as CEO of Palm, Inc. and cofounding Handspring with Jeff Hawkins in 1995.
- *Michael Eisner, English major from Denison University*: Eisner was the chairman and CEO of the Walt Disney Company from September 1984 to September 2005. Prior to Disney, Eisner was president and CEO of rival film studio Paramount

[18] Executive Bio on Timothy, M.D located at https://comparably.com/companies/sprint/timothy-m-donahue (accessed March 12, 2019).

Pictures from 1976 to 1984, and had brief stints at the major television networks: NBC, CBS, and ABC.

- *Carly Fiorina, History major from Stanford University*: Fiorina ran unsuccessfully for the U.S. Senate in 2010 and the Republican presidential nomination in 2016. As CEO of HP from 1999 to 2005, Fiorina was the first woman to lead a top-20 company as ranked by *Fortune* magazine. In 2002, Fiorina oversaw what was then the largest technology sector merger in history, in which HP acquired rival personal computer manufacturer, Compaq. The transaction made HP the world's largest seller of personal computers.
- *Kathryn Fuller, an English major from Brown University*: She is the chair of the National Museum of Natural History of the Smithsonian Institution. She served as chair of the Ford Foundation from May 2004 until October 2010. She was the president and chief executive officer of the World Wildlife Fund (WWF) from 1989 until July 2005.
- *Jeffrey R. Immelt, a math major from Dartmouth College*: He is an American business executive currently working as a venture partner at New Enterprise Associates. He retired as chairman of the board of the U.S.-based conglomerate General Electric on October 2, 2017. He was selected as GE's CEO by their board of directors in 2000 to replace Jack Welch upon Welch's retirement from GE.
- *Kimberly Kelleher, a history major from University of Wisconsin, Madison*: She serves as the publisher and chief revenue officer of Wired Ventures, LLC. Ms. Kelleher's career in media, marketing, and advertising spans over 20 years. Ms. Kelleher served as President of SAY Media, Inc. since 2012, where she oversaw the company's business strategy, including global sales, marketing, production, communications, media solutions, and content operations. Ms. Kelleher was worldwide publisher of *Time* magazine. During her tenure, she was named Advertising Age's Publisher of the Year in October 2011.
- *Donald. R. Knauss, a history major from Indiana University*: After college, Knauss enlisted in the Marines for four years and then

worked with Procter & Gamble. Knauss worked for Frito-Lay and Tropicana, mainly in marketing, although he also was head of the southeast sales department for Frito-Lay. Knauss was head of the North American operations of The Coca-Cola Company. In 2006, Knauss became the CEO of Clorox.

- *Michael Lynne, an English major from Brooklyn College*: After a chance encounter with law-school acquaintance Bob Shaye, Lynne joined New Line Cinema as outside legal counsel in the early 1980s. In 1990, he was appointed president and chief operating officer of the studio. In 2001, he was named cochairman and co-CEO.
- *John J. Mack, a history major from Duke University*: Mack worked at several firms around Wall Street before starting his career at Morgan Stanley in 1972 as a salesman and worked for the company for nearly thirty years rising steadily to positions of increasing responsibility. In March 1992, he assumed responsibility for Morgan Stanley's day-to-day operations as chairman of the operating committee. He was named president of Morgan Stanley in June 1993.
- *Samuel J. Palmisano, History major from Johns Hopkins University*: He was president and the eighth chief executive officer of IBM until January 2012. He also served as the chairman of the company until October 1, 2012. While in college he also played football (center, offensive tackle, team cocaptain) there, and turned down an opportunity to try out with the Oakland Raiders.
- *Herb Scannell, an English major from Boston College*: He is a Puerto Rican American media executive and businessman. He served as the president of Nickelodeon and TV Land from 1996 to 2006, was the founding CEO of Next New Networks, and the president of BBC Worldwide America. He served as the CEO of the Mitú Network until the summer of 2018. He became the president and CEO of KPCC-FM in January 2019.
- *Florence Steinberg, a history major from University of Massachusetts, Amherst*: She was an American publisher of one of the

first independent comic books, the underground/alternative comics hybrid Big Apple Comix, in 1975. Additionally, as the secretary for Marvel Comics editor Stan Lee and the fledgling company's receptionist and fan liaison during the 1960s Silver Age of Comic Books, she was a key participant of and witness to Marvel's expansion from a two-person staff to a pop culture conglomerate.

CEOs and senior executives endorse the humanities as viable college majors because they understand firsthand how the liberal arts translate into the workplace. Slack's CEO Stewart Butterfield, who has an undergraduate degree in philosophy from Canada's University of Victoria, said, "studying philosophy taught me how to write really clearly and how to follow an argument all the way down, which is invaluable in running meetings."[19] Steve Yi, CEO of web advertising platform MediaAlpha, earned an interdisciplinary degree in East Asian Studies at Harvard University and proclaimed that the liberal arts train students to thrive in subjectivity and ambiguity and how to see every issue from multiple perspectives, an invaluable skill to have in the technology sector. Danielle Sheer, a vice president at Carbonite, a cloud backup service, who studied existential philosophy at George Washington University, echoed similar sentiments and said her humanities education helps her to consider a plethora of different options and outcomes in every situation. Christopher Connor often relied on his sociology degree from Ohio State University to understand the needs of his employees and customers at Sherman-Williams and noted, "I found a liberal arts education and studying philosophy, sociology and psychology really energizing."[20] With this in mind, higher education administrators and faculty need to help students understand there is no one perfect business executive pedigree. Doing so would go a long way demonstrating how the humanities are relevant to the 21st century workplace.

---

[19] Elizabeth, S. 2014. "Why Top Tech CEOs Want Employees With Liberal Arts Degrees." *Fast Company*, August 28.

[20] Elizabeth, S. 2014. "Why Top Tech CEOs Want Employees With Liberal Arts Degrees." *Fast Company*, August 28.

No One Business Executive Pedigree

Contrary to public belief, the perfect business executive pedigree does not exist. The research conducted by Elena Botelho and Kim Powell published in *The CEO Next Door: Based on a Breakthrough Study of over 2,600 Leaders* found no perfect pedigree for the CEO position. Individuals who achieve the CEO position often do it by making bold career moves over the course of their career that catapult them to the top. Botelho and Powell discovered three common types of career catapults: the smaller role move, the big leap, and inherit the mess situation. First, many CEOs took a smaller role at some point in their career. They may have started something new like launching a product within their company or moved to a smaller company to take on a greater set of responsibilities. Individuals used this opportunity to build something from the ground up and make a substantial impact. Others who landed in the corner office took the big leap and said yes to opportunities even when the role was well beyond anything they've done previously. Even if they did not feel fully prepared for the challenges ahead, they still said yes. Finally, the third most common way people catapult themselves to the CEO position is to inherit a big mess. It could be an underperforming business unit, a failed product, or a bankruptcy—any major problem for the business that needs to be fixed fast. Messy situations cry out for strong leadership. When faced with a crisis, emerging leaders have an opportunity to showcase their ability to assess a situation calmly, make decisions under pressure, take calculated risks, rally others around them, and persevere in the face of adversity. Through these career catapults, executives build the specific behaviors that set successful CEOs apart—including decisiveness, reliability, adaptability, and the ability to engage for impact—and they get noticed for their accomplishments. The catapults are so powerful that even people who never aspired to become CEO ultimately landed the position by pursuing one or more of these strategies.

When education is factored into the equation of elements involved with landing in the CEO position, no one major is better than another. One study revealed that one-third of all Fortune 500 CEOs have a liberal arts degree[21]

[21] Elizabeth, S. 2014. "Why Top Tech CEOs Want Employees With Liberal Arts Degrees." *Fast Company*, August 28.

and businesses are learning that grade point average (GPA) was an artificial measure of how successful the student could be on the job. In research published in *The Wall Street Journal,* Carol Hymowitz studied the career trajectories of senior executives and concluded: "getting to the corner office has more to do with leadership talent and a drive for success" than graduating with a specific degree from a prestigious university.[22] CEOs who have worked with hundreds of other senior executives throughout their career understand the nominal role a college major has when moving up the corporate ladder.[23] When considering the nuances involved with long-term earning potential, the research overwhelmingly illustrates that "perceptions of the variations in economic success among graduates in different majors are exaggerated. Given a student's ability, achievement, and effort, his or her earnings do not vary all that greatly with the choice of undergraduate major."[24]

Debra Humphreys and Patrick Kelly summarized research conducted for the American Association of Colleges and Universities (AAC&U) and noted the evidence "demonstrates that while science, math, and engineering majors earn more on average than do those with other degrees upon graduation, (engineering) over time liberal arts graduates close the earnings gap with those who majored in professional or pre-professional fields."[25] Another study found that history majors who pursued careers in business ended up earning, on average, almost as much as business majors by mid-career.[26] The humanities graduates who succeed in business understand their education has provided a set of essential skills from which to launch their career.

---

[22] Carol, H. 2006. "Any College Will Do." *Wall Street Journal,* September 18.

[23] Louis, L. 2010. "Accidental Moguls: College Majors of Top CEOs." *Bloomberg Business Week,* May 17.

[24] Zac, B. 2010. "Your College Major May Not be as Important as You Think." *The New York Times,* November 3.

[25] Association of American Colleges and Universities (AAC&U). 2013. "It Takes More than a Major: Employer Priorities for College Learning and Student Success: Overview and Key Findings." April 10.

[26] Zac, B. 2010. "Your College Major May Not be as Important as You Think." *The New York Times,* November 3.

Essential Skills

To help alleviate the understanding disconnect, higher education officials should also communicate the value of skills over degrees. As City University of New York professor *Ann Kirschner* tweeted as a reaction to the speech Ginni Tometty gave at the 2019 World Economic Forum: "If there were a Dow Jones ticker for college degrees, we'd be seeing a market correction today, as the_@IBM CEO says we need to hire for skills not diplomas."[27] The 2018 Bloomberg Next *study* "Building Tomorrow's Talent: Collaboration Can Close Emerging Skills Gap" found that employers are now more focused on interpersonal skills rather than GPA. And although a small number of institutions are releasing extracurricular transcripts that demonstrate a student's individual skills in addition to grades [28] this emphasis of skill over major will be a herculean challenge since colleges are organized into departments that often operate as independent silos. The mere mention of skills over degrees could send shockwaves through a campus. But the research remains very clear on the value of skills over majors and higher education institutions need to help students understand this. As the AAC&U noted, "93 percent of employers surveyed said that a demonstrated capacity to think critically, communicate clearly, and solve complex problems is more important than a job candidate's undergraduate major." [29]

Thus, humanities majors will continue to remain relevant for those employers looking to hire recent graduates who can think critically, communicate effectively, solve complex problems, and demonstrate other relevant skills as organizations look to achieve and sustain growth in dynamic, hypercompetitive, and ever-changing global marketplace. These

---

[27] Blumenstyk, G. 2019. "5 Takeaways From 24 Hours at a Major Teaching Conference." *The Chronicle of Higher Education*, January 29. https://chronicle.com/article/5-Takeaways-From-24-Hours-at/245564 (accessed February 15, 2019).

[28] Wood, S. 2018. "Recent Graduates Lack Soft Skills, New Study Reports." *Diverse Education*, August 3. https://diverseeducation.com/article/121784/ (accessed October 10, 2018).

[29] Association of American Colleges and Universities (AAC&U). 2013. "It Takes More than a Major: Employer Priorities for College Learning and Student Success: Overview and Key Findings." April 10.

are commonly referred to as soft skills, or noncognitive skills, but a more accurate term would be to label them *essential skills*. Research conducted by the National Association of Colleges and Employers (NACE) illustrates how most hiring managers care more about a job candidate's skills than they do about a college major.[30] In fact, business executives will tell you "that they don't care what a job candidate has majored in."[31] They want students who can think, communicate orally, write, and solve problems. One such business executive is billionaire Mark Cuban. During the February 2017 NBA All-Star Technology Summit in New Orleans, Dallas Mavericks owner Mark Cuban predicted that liberal arts majors will be needed as technology continues to disrupt today's in-demand jobs like software development and engineering.[32] As Cuban stated "when the data is being provided, you need a different perspective in order to get a different view so free thinkers can provide that skill."[33]

Given the extremely rapid progress taking place in technologies causing disruption in almost every market, people in all lines of work should strive to be flexible about acquiring new skills and even about changing their occupations.[34] Enter the humanities majors and graduates. History, English, philosophy, and other humanities majors will provide the flexibility of mind, the multiplicity of perspectives, and the capacity of collaboration and innovation organizations need as they look to remain relevant. Cuban's observation falls in line with most surveys involving senior executives. Cuban is far from alone is his declaration that humanities majors will remain relevant to the 21st century workplace. In his editorial "A CEO's Advice to a Millennial: A Liberal Arts Degree Matters," retired

---

[30] Elka, T. 2018. "Employment Outlook for Graduate-Level Occupations." *Bureau of Labor Statistics*, August.

[31] Menegay, M.M. No Date. "Liberal Arts Is Slang For Job Skills." *Ask The Headhunter.com*, Located at http://asktheheadhunter.com/gv980429.htm

[32] Renee, M. 2017. "Why Mark Cuban Believes Liberal Arts Is The Future of Jobs." *Forbes*, February 28.

[33] Renee, M. 2017. "Why Mark Cuban Believes Liberal Arts Is The Future of Jobs." *Forbes*, February 28.

[34] Mangelsdorf, M.E. 2015. "The New World of Work." *MIT Sloan Management Review Magazine*, March 16.

CEO Edward Speed stressed just how valuable skills are for employers in evaluating humanities graduates when he wrote:

> Successful CEO's have little need for more graduates who tell senior management what the numbers say. What is desperately lacking are those who can tell management what the numbers mean. Data is cheap; gleaning information from data is rare; discerning meaning from information is priceless.[35]

Doing so requires the skill of critical thinking and not the degree of a specific major.

> Graduates who can connect the dots are sorely lacking, yet are needed more than ever in a world awash in overwhelming data. Senior executives desperately need on their team those who can read and listen critically, think and analyze analogically, and then communicate metaphorically to diverse internal and external stakeholders.[36]

The Conference Board's 2018 report "C-Suite Challenge" noted that the top two concerns of CEOs today are attracting and retaining talent and relying on that talent to create new business models because of disruptive technologies.[37] The competition for talent is as fierce as ever, as the global population ages, the nature of work changes, and companies look for the skills they need to nurture—now and in the future. In another survey 77 percent of CEOs interviewed voiced concern that skills shortages could hinder their organization's growth. Despite greater automation in the workforce, CEOs realize they can't rely on digital skills alone. To innovate, they need good problem-solvers and people with creative skills and high emotional intelligence. These are also the hardest skills to find.

---

[35] Edward, S. 2016. "A CEO's Advice to a Millennial: A Liberal Arts Degree Matters." *Rivard Report,* February 8.

[36] Edward, S. 2016. "A CEO's Advice to a Millennial: A Liberal Arts Degree Matters." *Rivard Report,* February 8.

[37] The Conference Board. 2018. "C-Suite Challenge 2018." January 18.

As LRN's chief executive Dov Seidman explains it, companies and leaders that recognize and put the human connection at the center of their strategy will be the enduring winners.[38] Indeed, "machines can be programmed to do the next thing right. But only humans can do the next right thing."[39]

When it comes to advising college students on how best to prepare for a future of work based on uncertainty, what do executives suggest? Research conducted on behalf of the AAC&U concluded that 80 percent of employers agree that, regardless of their major, every college student should acquire broad knowledge in the liberal arts and sciences through a liberal education.[40] The National Leadership Council echoed similar sentiment and concluded that "narrow preparation in a single area is exactly the opposite of what graduates need from college."[41] "When companies are assessing job candidates, they're looking for the best of both worlds: someone who is not only proficient in a particular function, but also has the right personality," said Rosemary Haefner, Vice President of Human Resources at CareerBuilder.

With this in mind, it is important for colleges and university leaders to recognize the value of both academic and technical education. As Janet Bray, Executive Director of the Association for Career and Technical Education, noted, "We need to move away in this country from either academic or career and technical education. It's not an either–or situation."[42] The basic academic skills include areas such as math and English, but schools shouldn't stop at teaching them—they must show students how to use academic knowledge in authentic situations they

---

[38] Bob, M. 2017. "Four Concerns that Keep CEOs Awake at Night." *CNBC*, January 18.

[39] Thomas, F. 2017. "From Hands to Heads to Hearts." *The New York Times*, January 4.

[40] Association of American Colleges and Universities (AAC&U). 2013. "It Takes More than a Major: Employer Priorities for College Learning and Student Success: Overview and Key Findings." April 10.

[41] Johnson, C.S. Spring 2012. "From the Editor." *Peer Review*, Vol 14. American Association of Colleges and Universities.

[42] Gerwetz, C. 2010. "Advocates Push New Definition of Career Readiness." *Education Week*, April 15.

might face. "Whether you're going to be a doctor, a lawyer, a welder, a nurse, a cosmetologist, you name it, you're going to need a core of academics that you can apply," Bray said. They also need to communicate effectively, work with others, and be creative. Students might be able to land a job, but they may not keep the job without these skills, said Dave Bunting, executive director of the Iowa Association for Career and Technical Education and former executive director of programs at Kirkwood Community College. "While employers want outstanding technical and academic skills, they absolutely demand outstanding employability skills," Bunting said.[43]

Conclusion

For the foreseeable future, executives will endorse the humanities and hiring managers will emphasize skills and internships over academic majors. Therefore, the humanities will remain relevant to the 21st century workforce. To support the humanities higher education institutions should address the comprehension disconnect. Such a process would involve helping those inside and outside of higher education understand the value of the humanities. Faculty can use resources such as the Andrew W. Mellon Foundation's 2019 report that examined the economic payoff of a liberal arts education. The study disproves that a liberal arts degree isn't worth its cost or will hurt a graduate's career prospects.

> Critics claim that a liberal arts education is worth less than the alternatives, and perhaps not even worth the investment at all. They argue that increasing costs and low future earnings limit the value of a liberal arts education. Existing evidence does not support these conclusions.[44]

---

[43] Roscorla, T. 2010. "Education Experts Define Career Readiness." *College and Career*, April 14.

[44] Hill, C.B., and E.D. Pisacreta. 2019. "The Economic Benefits and Costs of a Liberal Arts Education." January 2019. https://mellon.org/resources/news/articles/economic-benefits-and-costs-liberal-arts-education/ (accessed May 1, 2019).

Addressing the comprehension disconnect will involve a commitment to think differently by boards, presidents, and faculty. As the world grows ever more dynamic, hypercompetitive, and disruptive, thinking differently is perhaps the most critical skill to help the humanities remain relevant in the 21st century.

Technological advancements will present new forms of disruption, challenge old assumptions, and demand creative solutions. Innovations in artificial intelligence, drones, robotics, self-driving automobiles, and other technology will continue to disrupt many industries. To respond to such disruption, the humanities will be called upon to address new questions, issues, and problems associated with the 21st century workforce. As *The New York Times* editorialist Nicholas Kristof informed readers,

> Our world is enriched when coders and marketers dazzle us with smartphones and tablets, but, by themselves, they are just slabs. It is the music, essays, entertainment and provocations that they access, spawned by the humanities that animate them—and us. So, yes, the humanities are still relevant in the 21st century.[45]

Researcher Vivek Wadhwa echoed similar sentiment and observed that "the key to good design is a combination of empathy and knowledge of the arts and humanities."[46] Teaching artists hard skills such as math remains far easier than teaching engineers how to be creative. "Tackling today's biggest social and technological challenges requires the ability to think critically about their human context, which is something that

---

45 Kristof, N. 2014. "Don't Dismiss the Humanities." *The New York Times*, August 13.

46 Wadhwa, V. 2018. "Why Liberal Arts and the Humanities are as Important as Engineering." *The Washington Post*, June 12. https://washingtonpost.com/news/innovations/wp/2018/06/12/why-liberal-arts-and-the-humanities-are-as-important-as-engineering/?noredirect=on&utm_term=.128ec50ffca9 (accessed December 12, 2018).

humanities graduates happen to be best trained to do."[47] The research is overwhelmingly clear that

> employers want college graduates with already developed professional skills, and they won't necessarily take chances on candidates who cannot exhibit an aptitude for critical thinking, communication, and writing skills. Bridging the skill gap can occur long before students graduate and begin their job search. Institutions can invest in their graduates' futures by encouraging them to learn and demonstrate these vital professional skills in an academic setting prior to graduation.[48]

If higher education institutions can address the comprehension disconnect, the humanities majors will indeed remain relevant to the 21st century. Once boards, presidents, faculty, and other stakeholders address the comprehension disconnect, they can turn their attention toward the translation disconnect.

---

[47] Wadhwa, V. 2018. "Why Liberal Arts and the Humanities are as Important as Engineering." *The Washington Post,* June 12. https://washingtonpost.com/news/innovations/wp/2018/06/12/why-liberal-arts-and-the-humanities-are-as-important-as-engineering/?noredirect=on&utm_term=.128ec50ffca9 (accessed December 12, 2018)

[48] 2019. *Humanities and Social Science Majors Please Apply: Focusing on Liberal Arts Helps Students Get Jobs.*

CHAPTER 3

The Translation Disconnect

> Evolution in our careers is one of the most important things to learn and apply simultaneously as we earn. Without that, there is no door for growth.
>
> —Goitsemang Mvula

Introduction

Since long-term financial stability via employment is the overwhelming reason individuals seek a college degree, today's conventional wisdom has students declaring majors in health care, business, engineering and computer science. The belief held by many is that these majors have better employment prospects and higher earnings than those who choose a liberal arts such as English, history, or philosophy. While this may be true for the initial job secured following graduation, the long-term story is more complicated. As David Deming, noted in *The New York Times* "The advantage for STEM (science, technology, engineering and mathematics) majors fades steadily after their first jobs, and by age 40 the earnings of people who majored in fields like social science or history have caught up."[1] One of the reasons for this is because recent college graduates make the mistake of assuming their degree is synonymous with career preparedness. Research suggests otherwise and points to the next disconnect surrounding translation.

> The central issue in realizing a long-term strategy for student career development is *translation*. That is, how students translate the skills they learn during their college years, both in and out of

---

[1] David Deming. 2019. "In the Salary Race, Engineers Spring but English Majors Endure." *The New York Times*, September 20, 2019.

the classroom into workplace success. This is particularly true in the case of the metacognitive skills that professors in the humanities can, and should, help contribute in their students.

But most higher education institutions fail to provide the necessary support regarding the translation of one's undergraduate or graduate experience to the 21st century workplace. My previous book *Marketing Your Value: 9 Steps to Navigate Your Career* explains how college students and even more experienced professionals need to diligently and consistently demonstrate their value to employers. Doing so requires substantial work if any humanities major or graduate wants to remain relevant in the 21st century workforce. Humanities majors need to translate their academic, professional, and cocurricular experiences into a clear, concise, and compelling story so that prospective employers will pay attention. To that end, higher education institutions have a responsibility to help humanities majors with such a translation process. Unfortunately, much work needs to be done here. In a world where return on investment is carefully promoted as a key attribute for attending college, translating one's experiences to help launch a career remains a significant untapped strategy colleges can employ. Humanities majors would serve themselves well to remember what Thomas Friedman wrote in a January 25, 2012, *New York Times* editorial: "Being average just won't earn you what it used to. Everyone needs to find their unique value contribution that makes them stand out in whatever is their field of employment. Average is over." [2]

Explaining the Disconnect

While Chapter 1 discussed the explanation disconnect and Chapter 2 outlined the understanding disconnect, this chapter highlights the critical translation disconnect. The lack of support in helping humanities students translate their education and experience to launch their career or find employment remains the most significant issue facing humanities departments in higher education institutions today. It is the responsibility of everyone on campus to help humanities students translate their education and experience into a compelling story they can leverage as they

[2] Friedman, T.L. 2012. "Average Is Over." *The New York Times*, January 24.

launch their career. Unfortunately many faculty, staff, and administrators at most institutions believe "the value of liberal arts education can be hard to convey because it can't be boiled down to a simple sound bite or an eye-popping starting salary."[3] That is simply unacceptable today. It is equally unacceptable to rely on the time-honored tradition of relying on the inherent value argument where studying the liberal arts "benefits our souls, the way we view the world, and our innate creativity."[4]

A 2019 Emsi report concluded that higher education is not keeping pace with the ever-changing job market. The report examines the "translation chasm" between the skills graduates of liberal arts programs have and the skills employers say they're looking for in an applicant. Turns out they're not all that different, but "liberal arts graduates are too often left to stumble upon the valuable mixture of layered skills" required for any specific career, according to the report.[5] While many reports suggest that students should focus on studying marketable skills, the new report identifies career value in liberal arts education, albeit with some tweaks.[6] Created by Emsi, a labor market analytics firm, and the Strada Institute for the Future of Work, the report is based on more than 100 million social and professional profiles and applicant résumés and more than 36 million job postings to determine how to bridge the gap between what liberal arts students learn and what employers want.[7]

---

[3] Krislov, M. 2007. "The Life-Shaping Power of Higher Education." *Inside Higher Ed*, October 6, (Accessed April 8, 2019).

[4] Morrissey, S. Spring 2013. "The Value of a Liberal Arts Education." *Philosophy, Politics, and Economics Undergraduate Journal* 6, https://repository.upenn.edu/cgi/viewcontent.cgi?article=1041&context=spice (accessed April 10, 2019).

[5] *The Real, Long-term Labor Market Outcomes of Liberal Arts Grads.* November 2018 report published by Emsi and the Strada Institute for the Future of Work. https://economicmodeling.com/robot-ready-reports/ (accessed January 12, 2019).

[6] *The Real, Long-term Labor Market Outcomes of Liberal Arts Grads.* November 2018 report published by Emsi and the Strada Institute for the Future of Work. https://economicmodeling.com/robot-ready-reports/ (accessed January 12, 2019).

[7] *The Real, Long-term Labor Market Outcomes of Liberal Arts Grads.* November 2018 report published by Emsi and the Strada Institute for the Future of Work. https://economicmodeling.com/robot-ready-reports/ (accessed January 12, 2019).

Rob Sentz, chief innovation officer at Emsi, believes that "deans, administrators working in program development, institutional research departments and faculty advisers should all be focused on helping students translate what they are learning into skills that the labor market needs and wants." [8] Translating what they are learning into relevant skills for the 21st century workplace requires students to communicate their value by creating a clear, concise, and compelling set of marketing materials. Recognizing that many employers are unhappy or disengaged from their work, one observer noted: "It's no wonder many of us aren't fully satisfied with where we're at professionally. We keep ignoring that crucial personal component that helps drive great results."[9] It is time that higher education institutions pay attention to that crucial personal component of a student's undergraduate experience. To develop that crucial personal component, and to succeed in the job market of today and tomorrow, workers across all industries and titles will need to engage in a great deal of self-reflection. Doing so will allow people to get better at the skills of human interaction. As Geoff Colvin noted in *Humans Are Underrated: What High Achievers Know that Brilliant Machines Never Will*, workers need to "become champions at the skills of human interaction-empathy above all, social sensitivity, collaboration, storytelling, solving problems together, and building relationships." To demonstrate how one champions the skill of human interaction, it is imperative that all college students and recent graduates have a clear, concise, and compelling story. Doing so is an effective way to address the translation disconnect and an absolute necessity if students from any major are going to succeed in today's volatile, uncertain, complex, and ambiguous (VUCA) marketplace.

Higher education institutions need to do a far better job of helping humanities majors, as well as majors in other subjects, translate their value to the marketplace. To address this translation disconnect, colleges and universities can help humanities majors translate their value

---

[8] *The Real, Long-term Labor Market Outcomes of Liberal Arts Grads*. November 2018 report published by Emsi and the Strada Institute for the Future of Work. (accessed January 12, 2019).

[9] Bowen, J. 2015. "The Link Between Personal Development and Professional Success." *Huffington Post*, March 4.

to the marketplace via a clear, concise, and compelling story by implementing four strategies. First, colleges need to help students uncover the one word that would serve as the focus of their personal story. Second, institutions should teach humanities majors how to develop their value proposition—a statement of less than seven words that illustrates their current position in the marketplace. Third, schools should assist humanities majors in defining their success factors so they can place them at the top of their résumé and use them in interviews. Finally, colleges and universities need to provide opportunities for humanities majors to craft a personal statement that summarizes how their skills, knowledge, and experiences are relevant to the workplace.

Identify Your One Word

The first step in creating a compelling story is identifying your one word. Describing yourself in one word is one of the most difficult challenges to complete. If you do it correctly, however, it provides the focus you need as you start to learn how to communicate your value in a clear, concise, and compelling manner. The selection of a one-word descriptor is so important to the interview process and one's ability to communicate their value that LinkedIn has launched an annual list of overused LinkedIn profile buzzwords.

Here's the 2018 top 10 list with the definition of each word followed by a brief explanation followed by "Instead of" then "Try" examples. Remember, when it comes to describing yourself, it's better to show and not tell. Telling someone how good you are is annoying. Showing someone how good you are is impressive. Let them tell you how good you are. The most you have to tell someone how good you are, the less chance you have of landing the job. And if they don't tell you how good you are, would you really want to work for a place that ignores your skills, knowledge, and experience?

1. *Specialize*: Concentrate on and become an expert in a particular subject or skill. "Specialize" barely registered as a used word until the early 20th century when the Industrial Revolution introduced the concept of specialized skills. During the last few years, this word has been used so often on LinkedIn it has lost most of its meaning.

a. *Instead of:* I specialize in market research.

b. *Try*: For over five years market research has been the focus point of my experience.

2. *Experienced*: The knowledge or skill acquired by experience over a period of time, especially that gained in a particular profession by someone at work. Everyone is experienced so why rely on such an overused word? Like all of the other words in this top 10, using it will fail to help you differentiate yourself from other candidates.

    a. *Instead of:* I am experienced in qualitative market research.

    b. *Try*: During the past five years my qualitative market research success has provided me with invaluable lessons.

3. *Skilled*: Having or showing the knowledge, ability, or training to perform a certain activity or task well. This is a new entry to the LinkedIn list in 2018. Much like experience, everyone has a skill so there is little value in using this word. Remember, in today's hyperconnected world, people need the shortest path possible to understand your value. Relying on overused words like skilled are only going to frustrate people.

    a. *Instead of:* I am skilled in pharmaceutical market research.

    b. *Try*: Market research surveys under my guidance have provided critical insights into the minds and behaviors of consumers for my pharmaceutical brand team clients.

4. *Leadership*: The action of leading a group of people or an organization. Perhaps no two terms get more confused than management and leadership. If you ask 10 people to define both terms, you will get a wide variety of answers. Therefore, when you use leadership, be clear as to your application; otherwise you leave interpretation up to the reader. Is that something you really want to do?

    a. *Instead of:* I have led over 12 market research projects.

    b. *Try:* My experience includes managing over 12 market research projects across three different product categories. Each project involved qualitative and quantitative metrics.

5. *Passionate*: Showing or caused by strong feelings or a strong belief; derived from passion meaning to suffer. Perhaps the most misused and misunderstood word on the list. The argument could be made that it is one of the most misunderstood words today. While passion-

ate is used to explain one's excitement for work, also known as purpose, it fails to offer any specific description about your capabilities.

a. *Instead of*: I am passionate about market research.

b. *Try*: Market research has fueled my career during the last 10 years and provided me with the ability to develop both personally and professionally.

6. *Expert*: A person who has a comprehensive and authoritative knowledge of or skill in a particular area. Everyone seems to be an expert about something today. Just ask them, they will tell you on social media. And since social media is so prolific they will remind you of how much they are an expert each and every day.

   a. *Instead of:* I am an expert in market research.

   b. *Try:* My publication record during the last 10 years includes three articles and five presentations regarding the advancements of technology and their impact on market research.

7. *Motivated*: Provide (someone) with a motive for doing something or you are highly self-motivated to accomplish a goal. A modern day buzz word that, like the other words on this list, provide little guidance for a stranger trying to figure out your value. What exactly does a motivated person look like? And who cares? You may be so motivated as to not follow directions or want to be a team member. Remember, for every definition of a word you have someone else may interpret it in an entirely different manner.

   a. *Instead of*: I am a motivated market researcher.

   b. *Try*: My high level of energy, dedication to the client, and ability to work with others all form the foundation of each market research project.

8. *Creative*: Relating to or involving the imagination or original ideas, especially in the production of an artistic work. The one word on this list that means nothing when you tell someone; you must show your creativity or it is meaningless. People mistake artists as those who have a monopoly on the use and application of the word creative. Nothing could be further from the truth. Everyone needs to be creative to some degree.

   a. *Instead of*: I am creative when it comes to market research findings.

b. *Try*: When identifying next steps and recommendations for my clients, I tend to offer both traditional and nontraditional ideas as to how they might address situations identified in the project.

9. *Strategic*: Relating to the identification of long-term or overall aims and interests and the means of achieving them. People tend to use this word to describe their ability to think through a situation. By using such a word, people hope to convey a level of sophistication in their thinking. Much like creative, it is an overused buzzword that does little to help people understand your thinking.
   a. *Instead of*: I am a strategic market researcher.
   b. *Try*: My findings in market research reports illustrate a variety of options that will allow the client to consider a spectrum of ideas designed to achieve one or more business objectives of the brand team.
10. *Focused*: To see clearly. In today's hyper-competitive, dynamic, and ever-changing global marketplace it is important to demonstrate that you can be focused to complete one task after another. Being too focused, however, could be interpreted that you spend far too much time trying to achieve perfection. Remember, perfection is often the enemy of the good so be careful when telling people you are focused. What exactly are you focused on and why?
    a. *Instead of*: I am focused on completing each market research project.
    b. *Try:* Over 90 percent of my market research projects get completed online and under budget due to my dedication to teamwork, organization, and profitability.

While there were similarities around the globe among these top 10 buzzwords, LinkedIn identified some notable outliers such as the word "sustainable" in the Netherlands; "enthusiastic" in Great Britain, and "passionate" in Australia and New Zealand.[10] If humanities majors and graduates are to remain relevant in the 21st century workplace, higher education institutions need to incorporate the translation of experience, knowledge, and skills into a clear, concise, and compelling personal story.

---

[10] Choi, C. 2013. "Top 10 Overused LinkedIn Profile Buzzwords of 2013." *LinkedIn article*, December 11.

Doing so will enable humanities graduates to explain their value during job interviews. Identifying their one-word descriptor is the first step in this process.

Identify Your One Word Exercise

Directions: Draw an inverted triangle with the large part at the top and the tip at the bottom. At the top part of the triangle, the largest section, write down 10 words you would use to describe yourself in the top section of the triangle. From those 10 select the top 5 and write them in the middle section. From those 5 select the one word you would use to describe yourself and write that in the bottom (smallest) section at the tip of the triangle.

Additional exercise: Ask 10 people to describe you in one word and compare their word against yours. Did most people have a similar word that you selected? If not, why do you think that is? If they are choosing a word that closely resembles the one word you choose than please recognize that you are positioning yourself well in the minds of others. This is an important realization as you move forward and market your value and navigate your career.

Value Proposition Exercise

Following the identification of the one-word descriptor, the next step in helping humanities majors translate their college experience into a compelling story is the development of a value proposition. A value proposition is a statement of seven words or less that help make the humanities graduate stand out from the competition. Think of a value proposition as a tagline that brands use. As *AdAge* described it, a tagline is an unforgettable phrase that perfectly encapsulates a brand promise.[11] Once found, a slogan can define a brand for decades. Here are the top 15 slogans for the 20th Century:

---

[11] 1999. "Ad Age Advertising Century: Top 10 Slogans." March 29, https://adage.com/article/special-report-the-advertising-century/ad-age-advertising-century-top-10-slogans/140156 (accessed May 22, 2019).

- "A diamond is forever"—DeBeers
- "Just do it"—Nike
- "The pause that refreshes"—Coca-Cola
- "Tastes great, less filling"—Miller Lite
- "We try harder"—Avis
- "Good to the last drop"—Maxwell House
- "Breakfast of champions"—Wheaties
- "Does she ... or doesn't she?"—Clairol
- "When it rains, it pours"—Morton Salt
- "Where's the beef?"—Wendy's
- "Look Ma, no cavities!"—Crest toothpaste
- "Let your fingers do the walking"—Yellow Pages
- "Loose lips sink ships"—public service
- "M&Ms melt in your mouth, not in your hand"—M&M candies
- "We bring good things to life"—General Electric

Yes, it's true that humanities majors and graduates are not consumer brands. Make no mistake that is not the implication here. But if humanities majors and graduates are to remain relevant in the 21st century, each individual will need to develop a one-word descriptor and a value proposition as effective tools to use during job interviews, networking events, or informal conversations about their potential value to an organization. Examples include: "How would you describe yourself in a minute or less?" "What is your greatest strength?" "Why should we hire you?" A clear, concise, and compelling value proposition contains the following design elements:

- *It highlights an ability to focus*: A value proposition is seven words or less because it forces the humanities major to focus on the quality of words, not quantity. It is impolite to ramble on for more than a few minutes when answering an interview question. During an interview, it is imperative to focus on what is most important and engaging in a conversation.
- *It demonstrates preparation*: A well-defined value proposition illustrates that you have given it some thought. The last thing

you want to do is stumble on such an important question during an interview or networking event.
- *It allows you to tell a story*: A compelling statement should help spark a conversation where you can then discuss how one or more of your experiences support the words you have chosen for your value proposition.

Examples of value propositions (each seven words or less):

- Using keen insight to help customers.
- Relying on resiliency to transform businesses.
- Inspiring people to pursue vibrant career paths.
- Focused on collaboration and leadership development.
- Achieving progress through passion and team work.
- Global marketer dedicated to new ideas and insights.
- Helping others develop a passion for affordable wine.
- Driving innovative product design through enthusiasm.
- Experienced senior executive focused on results.
- Building relationships through empathy and concern.
- An energy provider who gets things done.
- Developing human capital to move organizations forward.
- Growing profits by increasing effectiveness and efficiency.
- Creating compelling brands across different industries.
- Action-orientated professional driven to succeed.

Directions:

- Step 1: Write down at least five value proposition statements you would use to describe yourself.
- Step 2: Share your ideas with others and ask them if they believe any one of those statements best describes you. If you get a consensus you might want to use the one people agree upon. If not, you may need to draft a few more statements and rethink your word choice. This is a difficult exercise for many people since they stress over selecting the best words. The best thing to do is

use your value proposition for a while and see how people react to it. Remember you can always change it.

- Step 3: What value proposition did you decide to use?

Success Factors

Now that you have your one-word descriptor and a seven-word value proposition, you can turn your attention to identifying your success factors. With recruiters and hiring managers inundated on a daily basis with hundreds or thousands of applicants submitting their materials, they often resort to skimming résumés. They simply lack adequate time to read each résumé word-for-word. One study suggested that recruiters and hiring managers glace at your résumé for six seconds. Other research indicates that hiring managers and recruiters may spend between 30 seconds up to two minutes reading your résumé. Whether it's six seconds or two minutes, "that's hardly any time to impress someone who could determine your employment future."[12] If you are unable to keep their attention they will most likely toss your résumé aside. Let's review that last sentence. The operative phrase is "if you are unable to keep their attention." Please understand that while you may have spent hours crafting your résumé, it may still lack the compelling material a recruiter or hiring manager needs at that point in time. To help you grab someone's attention while they are reading your résumé, you may want to consider placing three to five success factors at the top of your first page.

Placing three to five success factors at the top of the first page of your résumé allows you to effectively market your value within seconds. "Research suggests that content elements that propel employers to immediately discard résumés include a focus on duties instead of accomplishments, while documented achievements were highly ranked among content elements that employers look for."[13] Since successful factors focus on accomplishments you are practicing, the trait of differentiating your

---

[12] Adams, S. 2014. "The Best and Worst Words to Use on Your Résumé." *Forbes*, March 17, 2014.

[13] Hansen, K. No Date. "Avoid These 10 Résumé Mistakes." *Quintessential Careers*.

value from the other candidates. By focusing on your accomplishments, you grab the reader's attention. Your success factors help them understand why they should call you for an interview. Success factors indirectly answer one or more of the following questions:

- What special things did this candidate do in their past that sets them apart from others?
- How well did you do your previous job?
- What specific results did you achieve in your current position?
- What were the problems or challenges that you or the organization faced and how did you overcome the problems?
- How did the company benefit from your performance?
- How did you leave your employers better off than before you worked for them?
- How have you helped your employers to:
  - make money
  - save money
  - save time
  - make work easier and more efficient
  - solve a specific problem
  - be more competitive
  - build relationships
  - expand the business
  - attract new customers
  - retain existing customers

Examples of Success Factors

- Managed and collaborated with writers, photographers, and editors to produce the campus section of *The Anchor*, Hope's student-managed newspaper, ensuring well written, carefully researched and edited news stories.
- Wrote stories that involved interviews, online research, and event coverage.
- Designed compelling layouts using Adobe InDesign and Photoshop.

- Worked as data analyst for a Fortune 100 company.
- Obtained a career center graduate assistantship at Grand Valley State University.
- Gained advising skills on three different levels: a private baccalaureate institution, a master's degree granting institution, and a level one research institution.
- Launched major plank of strategic plan.
- Oversaw a budget of $2 million and led a staff of 15.
- Presented at Michigan Career Personnel Association's (MCPA) Annual Conference, 2013.
- Managed a variety of situations in nonprofit and for-profit environments.
- Successfully increased sales by 17 percent for a product line within a 24 month period.

Directions: Write down at least three but no more than five success factors. You will eventually place these at the top of your résumé. For now, be sure to write down a few sentences that explain your evidence supporting each one of your success factors. You can then mention those during an interview or networking event.

Write Your Personal Statement

A personal statement is a summary of your professional skills, personal traits, and experiences in 75 words or less. Why the word limit? In today's never-ending stream of information employers have little time to read paragraphs about you and what you offer. They are busy. A brief personal statement of 75 words or less can help spark a conversation and that is your goal. You should be able to say your personal statement in 30 seconds or less. Remember, you need to do everything that you can to advocate for yourself while helping the prospective employer understand how you can help address the needs of the organization. Keeping your personal statement brief also allows you to engage others in the conversation. Let me give you an example of how this went very wrong for a recent candidate my friend interviewed.

During a recent interview for a position on my friend's team the candidate, let's call him Jon, was tasked to "Tell us about yourself." 10 minutes later, Jon ended his answer. After about one minute into his far too long of a reply, my friend stopped listening to Jon. Out of professional courtesy, my friend and his staff continued the interview but Jon failed to engage them in a conversation. You must maintain the highest levels of self-awareness during an interview or networking event in order to engage others. Having a concise, compelling, and clear personal statement is an excellent tool to use. While you will want to craft your credentials to each position you are applying to, it is imperative to have a general personal statement that you can plug into your personal web site as well as the Summary field of your LinkedIn profile. Here are several examples of personal statements.

- *Personal Statement Example #1*: With various experience in higher education, I am a disciplined and responsible young professional who is committed to excellence. Reliable and personable, I work well both individually and on teams. My passion lies in building relationships and collaborating with others. I am able to adapt effectively to any situation and establish positive environments with my outstanding communication and problem-solving skills. My ambitious attitude enables me to prioritize multiple tasks and take initiative. You can rely on me.
- *Personal Statement Example #2*: With diligence and motivation, I have dedicated myself to lifelong self-improvement both personally and professionally. My outstanding attention to quality and detail, together with my ability to prioritize, allows me to successfully complete independent and team-based projects through careful listening and effective communication. Over the course of my experiences I have demonstrated the ability of getting comfortable while uncomfortable by adapting to challenging situations, resolving issues through analytical and critical thinking and acting courageously.
- *Personal Statement Example #3*: As a determined and enthusiastic young professional, I strive to continuously inspire those

around me on a daily basis. Driven by my ambitious mindset, influential attitude, and synergistic appreciation, I find passion in communicating and collaborating with a variety of individuals to better reach success and achievement of goals. Through my possession of outstanding decision-making and problem-solving skills, I am able to adapt effectively to any stressful situation and better encourage feelings of positivity.

- *Personal Statement Example #4*: I am a motivated professional who acts as a catalyst. Through my ability to approach tasks with enthusiasm and a positive attitude, I have a proven strength in leadership. My capacity to take calculated risks propels improvement and drives advancement toward goals. I combine resourcefulness, determination, and problem-solving strategies to create innovative plans of action, which I am able to carry out with my oral and written communication abilities.
- *Personal Statement Example #5*: Trustworthy and dependable, I am a self-starter with a passion for learning about the world and connecting with people. Through written and verbal communication, I am eager to form and nurture relationships in the professional world. My work in journalism, the nonprofit sector, and college admissions has displayed my effective interpersonal skills and pursuit of quality communication.
- *Personal Statement Example #6*: As a versatile, dependable, and responsible professional I enjoy working with nonprofit organizations and small businesses. Collaboration with others and personal growth are the hallmarks of my background. Becoming a reliable, adaptable, and ambitious individual has led to an increased skill set in communications, publishing, and marketing. Through my internships and employment positions, I have developed a strong sense of leadership in helping others solve problems, answer questions, and address issues.
- *Personal Statement Example #7*: As a smart, hardworking, and driven individual, I work to achieve success through commitment while communicating my ideas to others and working with them to achieve our shared goals. When problems arise, I am able to think critically and analyze the situation in order

to come to an effective situation. My work with children has provided me with an opportunity to create my own life and in turn support others in their efforts to do the same.

- *Personal Statement Example #8*: As a professional who displays energy in performing daily responsibilities, I am a motivated and engaged individual. I can adapt to challenging situations, work independently, and successfully complete individual and team projects. My professional background includes a variety of experiences that have allowed me to demonstrate my dedication to self-improvement and commitment to excellence. With a willingness to learn, coupled with an ability to take calculated risks I strive for perfection while addressing challenges.

Conclusion

Once a humanities major has created a clear, concise, and compelling story to translate their college experience, they will then need to communicate it online via a web site. According to *Workfolio*, a newly launched company that develops applications for professional visibility, 56 percent of all hiring managers are more impressed by a candidate's personal website than any other personal branding tool—however, less than 10 percent of job seekers actually have a personal website.[14] Approximately 30 percent of employers said a personal website can create a competitive advantage in the job market; and 39 percent said—all other qualifications being equal—they would be likelier to pick a candidate with a personal website over a candidate without one.[15] Workfolio's founder and chief executive

[14] Smith, J. 2013. "Why Every Job Seeker Should Have A Personal Website, And What It Should Include." *Forbes*, April 26 https://forbes.com/sites/jacquelynsmith/2013/04/26/why-every-job-seeker-should-have-a-personal-website-and-what-it-should-include/#5941b3b3119e

[15] Zetlin, M. 2015. "Do This One Thing to Stand Out From 99 Percent of Job Candidates." *Inc*, August 3. https://inc.com/minda-zetlin/do-this-one-thing-to-stand-out-from-99-percent-of-job-candidates-infographic.html

Charles Pooley knows how "the employment market is an incredibly scary place to be right now as a job seeker and a personal website offers candidates the creative freedom to express their personality in ways that are not be possible through a resume."[16] To stand out from the crowd, and to remain relevant, humanities majors need to have their own web site. Doing so provides a platform that allows humanities majors to illustrate how they have translated their college experience into a clear, concise, and compelling story. Louise Parker, 25, a University of Birmingham graduate, says her online presence was particularly important as she was applying for jobs in the digital industry. According to Parker, "Not only does it give you something to talk about on your application or in your interview, it also shows initiative and dedication."[17] The same can be said for a compelling social media presence.

According to a 2018 CareerBuilder survey, 70 percent of employers use social media to screen candidates during the hiring process.[18] Therefore, social media offers an excellent platform for humanities majors to tell employers about their skills, knowledge, and experience. After the humanities major creates a personal website, they can then add that URL to social media sites such as LinkedIn, Facebook, Instagram, and Twitter just to name a few. In the 21st century hiring process humanities majors want to know how prospective candidates represent themselves appropriately across various social media platforms. Having a personal website

---

[16] Smith, J. 2013. "Why Every Job Seeker Should Have A Personal Website, And What It Should Include." *Forbes*, April 26. https://forbes.com/sites/jacquelynsmith/2013/04/26/why-every-job-seeker-should-have-a-personal-website-and-what-it-should-include/#5941b3b3119e

[17] Smith, J. 2013. "Why Every Job Seeker Should Have A Personal Website, And What It Should Include." *Forbes*, April 26. https://forbes.com/sites/jacquelynsmith/2013/04/26/why-every-job-seeker-should-have-a-personal-website-and-what-it-should-include/#5941b3b3119e

[18] Career Builder Press Release, "More Than Half of Employers Have Found Content on Social Media That Caused Them NOT to Hire a Candidate, According to Recent CareerBuilder Survey." August 9, 2018, https://prnewswire.com/news-releases/more-than-half-of-employers-have-found-content-on-social-media-that-caused-them-not-to-hire-a-candidate-according-to-recent-careerbuilder-survey-300694437.html

and a social media presence that presents a clear, concise, and compelling presentation of skills, experiences, and success factors will go a long way in helping humanities majors remain relevant to the 21st century workplace. Doing so will also position a humanities major for a wide variety of available career options. Three career paths based on knowledge, issues, and skills provide numerous opportunities for humanities majors. Such vision requires higher education institutions to address the disconnect surrounding how students are educated around career opportunities.

CHAPTER 4

The Perception Disconnect

> One of the most compelling findings in this year's Global CEO Outlook is that over two-thirds of chief executive officers believe that agility is the new currency of business. If they fail to adapt to a constantly changing world, their business will become irrelevant.[1]
>
> —2019 KPMG *Agile or Irrelevant* Report

Introduction

The next disconnect concerns the perception related to career opportunities for humanities majors and graduates. For far too long liberal arts graduates are often told that if they are unable to find work as a teacher they will end up as taxi drivers, coffee baristas, or bartenders. With "useless degrees" no one will want to hire them. Nothing could be further from the truth. This disconnect over the perception of career opportunities is the leading reason why the number of humanities majors has decreased during the last few decades. More specifically, the inability of college administrators, faculty, and staff to help students and graduates understand the wide variety of career opportunities is the leading reason why the number of majors has decreased. Unless this disconnect is addressed immediately and effectively, the number of humanities majors will only continue to spiral downward. Administrators, faculty, and staff need to think differently, have a sense of urgency, and illustrate the myriad of career opportunities available to humanities majors. This is especially true in today's return-on-investment (ROI) driven society.

---

[1] KPMG. 2019. "Agile or Irrelevant: Redefining Resilience." Global CEO Outlook.

The latest student loan debt statistics for 2019 show how serious the student loan debt crisis has become for borrowers across all demographics and age groups. There are more than 44 million borrowers who collectively owe $1.5 trillion in student loan debt in the United States alone. Student loan debt has become the second highest consumer debt category—behind only mortgage debt—and scores higher than both credit cards and auto loans. Borrowers in the Class of 2017, on average, owe $28,650, according to the Institute for College Access and Success.[2] Choosing a college degree with the highest possible return on a student's investment is becoming more of a priority. As emerging technologies rapidly and thoroughly transform the workplace, some experts predict that 400 to 800 million people worldwide could be displaced and will need to find new jobs by 2030. The ability to adapt and quickly acquire new skills will become a necessity for survival.[3] "Too often, degrees are still thought of as lifelong stamps of professional competency. They tend to create a false sense of security, perpetuating the illusion that work—and the knowledge it requires—is static. It's not."[4]

To achieve and sustain career success during the 2020s and beyond humanities majors and graduates need to become more agile in their thinking, approach to careers, and skill development. Agility is derived from the Latin *agilitās* meaning nimble, fleet, or quick. Regardless of career position, status, or title, it will behoove individuals to improve their agility as the world continues to adapt to disruptive technologies. Since two-thirds of chief executive officers believe that agility is the new currency of business those who fail to demonstrate flexibility risk their organization becoming irrelevant.[5] Rapid technological advancements

---

[2] Zack, F. 2019. "Student Loan Debt Statistics In 2019: A $1,5 Trillion Crisis." *Forbes*, February 25. https://forbes.com/sites/zackfriedman/2019/02/25/student-loan-debt-statistics-2019/#825619f133fb (accessed April 16, 2019).

[3] Sarah, G. 2018. "Students are being Prepared for Jobs that No Longer Exist. Here's How that Could Change." *NBC News*, April 12. https://nbcnews.com/news/us-news/students-are-being-prepared-jobs-no-longer-exist-here-s-n865096 (accessed April 16, 2019).

[4] Stephane, K. 2018. "The Future of Work Won't be About College Degrees, It Will be About Job Skills." *CNBC*, October 31

[5] KPMG. 2019. "Agile or Irrelevant: Redefining Resilience." Global CEO Outlook.

will continue into the next decade driving the need for workers to increase their flexibility. As computer programmers develop new algorithms to automate current manual tasks workers need to stay agile and commit to lifelong learning in order to develop new skills, identify new career paths, and consider new occupations.[6]

Explaining the Disconnect

The lack of college faculty with employment experience outside of the academy, the shifting reliance on college degrees by employers, and inadequate career service offices are the three main contributing factors to the perception disconnect. More than 80 percent of students cite the prospect of a job as a critical factor in their decision to enroll in college.[7] Unfortunately, once they're enrolled, only a few students feel confident in their ability to participate in the job market and the workplace (34 and 36 percent, respectively).[8] Part of the reason for this lack of confidence stems from the fact that many instructors lack professional work experience outside of higher education and struggle to help humanities majors identify career opportunities. Humanities departments place a premium on learning while relegating the connection to employment opportunities a distant second. It's no surprise then that the number of humanities majors continues to decline. It's true that academia has a bias toward formal credentials, but it is equally true to remember that a PhD by itself does not

---

[6] MacCrory, F., G. Westerman, Y. Alhammadi, and E. Brynjolfsson. 2014. "Racing With and Against the Machine: Changes in Occupational Skill Composition in an Era of Rapid Technological Advance." Thirty Fifth International Conference on Information Systems, Auckland.

[7] Eagan, K., E.B. Stolzenberg, J.J. Ramirez, M.C. Aragon., M.R. Suchard, and C. Rios-Aguilar. 2016. "The American Freshman: Fifty-Year Trends, 1966–2015, Cooperative Institutional Research Program at the Higher Education Research Institute at UCLA." https://heri.ucla.edu/monographs/50YearTrendsMonograph2016.pdf (accessed April 16, 2019).

[8] The Strada-Gallup 2017 College Student Survey. 2019. "Crisis of Confidence: Current College Students Do Not Feel Prepared for the Workforce." https://news.gallup.com/reports/225161/2017-strada-gallup-college-student-survey.aspx (accessed April 16, 2019).

necessarily certify someone as capable of effective instruction. "Teaching quality is not actually part of what is judged for the credential. The PhD is a certification of significant scholarly achievement, but not so much effective teaching."[9]

This scholarly achievement, while necessary for promotion and tenure purposes, seldom melds with what is actually going on in the world. It is surprising how many faculty members have no work or management experience outside the confines of their academic institutions. Part of the reason for this is that they choose not to gain industry exposure in favor of pursuing an academic career. Once a faculty member gains tenure, which is a guaranteed job and pension for life, then there is little incentive for them to find another employment position. Perhaps nowhere is this more evident than in business schools and classes. As one observer noted "It is ridiculous that seasoned managers in executive MBA programmes are often taught by people who have zero experience of making the challenging decisions their own students grapple with regularly."[10]

The second factor contributing to the perception disconnect is the shift from solely relying on a college degree as the prerequisite for employment. "When you look at people who don't go to school and make their way in the world, those are exceptional human beings. And we should do everything we can to find those people," said Laszlo Bock, Google's former SVP of people operations. "Academic qualifications will still be taken into account and indeed remain an important consideration when assessing candidates as a whole, but will no longer act as a barrier to getting a foot in the door," added Maggie Stilwell, Ernst and Young's managing partner for talent.[11] Companies that do not require a college degree now include:

---

[9] Warner, J. 2017. "Credentials? Experience? Expertise? Who Gets to Teach?" *Inside Higher Ed*, May 4.

[10] Tse, T., and M. Esposito. 2014. "Academia is Disconnected from the Real World." *Financial Times*, March 30. https://ft.com/content/4f5fc7a2-7861-11e3-831c-00144feabdc0 (accessed March 22, 2019).

[11] 2015. "G15 More Companies That No Longer Require A Degree-Apply Now." *Glassdoor*, August 14. https://glassdoor.com/blog/no-degree-required/ (accessed April 16, 2019).

1. Google
2. EY
3. Penguin Random House
4. Costco Wholesale
5. Whole Foods
6. Hilton
7. Publix
8. Apple
9. Starbucks
10. Nordstrom
11. Home Depot
12. IBM
13. Bank of America
14. Chipotle
15. Lowe's

Remember, this section addresses the perception that humanities majors can only do certain jobs, most of which are useless. This is completely false. While 65 percent of jobs require postsecondary education, managers still consider internships, employment during college, and volunteer experience more important than grade point average (GPA) or relevant coursework when evaluating a candidate's readiness for a job. In short, the real world doesn't care about your degree as much as your work ethic, ability to fit into the culture, and willingness to learn. Colleges need to inform their students of this expectation but seldom will because such a message relegates the institution to a secondary position. In today's hypercompetitive marketplace, colleges and universities need to do everything they can in order to recruit students and stay afloat financially. Marketing a message that the school is secondary to a student's career path would only jeopardize the institution's recruitment strategy. If faculty are unable to provide reality based career advice, it is then up to the career services department to educate students. Unfortunately these offices often lack the resources, personnel and level of sophistication required and contribute to the perception disconnect that humanities majors can only apply to certain jobs.

According to data from a Gallup-Purdue University Survey recent college graduates were more likely than those in prior decades to visit a career center while in college but are less likely to view their interactions as "very helpful." Only 17 percent of those who graduated from 2010 to 2016 said they found their college career centers to be "very helpful," with another 26 percent reporting that the career office was "helpful."[12] That's compared to 35 percent of students who graduated five decades ago and 55 percent of students who graduated between 2000 and 2009.[13] The findings suggest it's not enough for a college to simply offer career services, said Brandon Busteed, who leads Gallup's education work. "This is very much about the quality of those interactions."[14] Moreover, engineering and business majors are the most likely to visit career services offices while arts and humanities and science majors, the least. How can an institution address the perception disconnect if humanities majors use the career services office the least? Well, there are numerous strategies available for use if an institution is committed to helping students understand that the humanities majors are relevant to the twenty-first century workplace.

If the humanities are to maintain relevance in the 21st century workplace administrators, faculty, and staff need to provide students and graduates with a different perspective on the many career opportunities available. Addressing this perception disconnect requires higher education institutions to help humanities majors expand their career horizons by implementing the three-career-path approach to professional development. Leveraging all of the career opportunities related to the three career paths paradigm is even more relevant given the fact that today's college students will experience an average of 11.9 career changes over their lifetimes, half of which will occur between the ages of 18 to 24.[15] Calling for "colleges to partner with business and industry to develop the skills that will prepare students for a future

---

[12] New, J. 2016. "Looking for Career Help." *Inside Higher Ed*, December 13.

[13] New, J. 2016. "Looking for Career Help." *Inside Higher Ed*, December 13.

[14] Zinshteyn, M. 2016. "New Poll: College Grads Unhappy with the Career Services they're Getting." *Hechinger Report*, December 13.

[15] 2019. "Number of Jobs, Labor Market Experience, and Earnings Growth: Results from a National Longitudinal Survey." *Bureau of Labor Statistics*, August 22.

none of us can fully predict" is a noble idea but it is merely just one tactic.[16] And since higher education institutions implement change at a glacial pace, it really is up to the students and graduates to leverage the three-career-path paradigm if they want to achieve and sustain career success. In short, to remain relevant to the twenty-first century workplace, humanities majors need to understand their options when it comes to employment opportunities. The first opportunity is the most common and the one spoken about frequently on college campuses and is known as the knowledge career path. The second path helps humanities majors find employment positions that are directly related to those issues most dear to their heart. Finally, the third career path provides a valuable alternative to humanities majors who want to leverage their skill set to land a job. Implementing the three-career-path approach will fail unless the institution is committed to educating students on the value of jobs outside of the academy for humanities majors. The percentage of undergraduates attending college to "get a better job" has risen from 72 percent a decade ago to 85 percent today.[17] If students are serious about getting a better job, then they need to challenge themselves to think about each of the three career paths. Doing so will help them navigate the chaos of landing a job that does not exist using technologies not yet invited to solve a problem not yet identified.

The Knowledge Career Path

Since higher education institutions are organized by academic departments, a model that has remained unchanged for centuries, the knowledge career path is the most common. This approach drives almost all of the marketing toward high school students considering college as a path to a lucrative career. In today's ROI driven marketplace, high school students are told to major in business, finance, or other careers that "pay well" and to steer away from those "low-paying" humanities majors. All too often the perception both inside and outside of higher education is that the

---

[16] 2019. "Yes, Employers Do Value Liberal Arts Degrees." *Harvard Business Review,* September 19.

[17] Greeley, M. 2019. "How Colleges Help Students Gear Up for Jobs." *U.S. News & World Report,* September 9.

knowledge career path is the only one available to humanities majors. For example, history majors can work in an archive, English majors can write, or philosophy majors can teach. This paradigm of career development remains a stable approach for many. Table 4.1 provides examples of knowledge jobs for a history major. This is not a comprehensive list but it does illustrate the most common knowledge based jobs for history majors. These employment positions rely on the candidate's knowledge, which is paramount to being competent in the job. Without this level of knowledge it would be difficult, if not impossible, to perform the required tasks the position demands.

It's unfortunate that far too many humanities majors feel as failures if they are unable to secure employment in their major. It's important to remember that the world is not organized by academic major. Therefore, finding a job that directly relates to your major is not a perquisite for success. In fact, the majority of opportunities fall far from the knowledge based career approach. In the knowledge based career paradigm

Table 4.1 Examples of knowledge jobs for a history major

Historians as Educators	Historians as Communicators
Elementary schools	Writers and editors
Secondary schools	Journalists
Postsecondary education	Documentary editors
Historic sites and museums	Producers of multimedia material
Historians as Information Managers	**Historians as Advocates**
Archivists	Lawyers and paralegals
Records Managers	Litigation support
Librarians	Legislative staff work
Information managers	Foundations
Historians in Businesses and Associations	**Historians as Researchers**
Historians in corporations	Museums and historical organizations
Historians and nonprofit associations	Historic preservation
	Think-tanks

humanities will also lose out to the "more profitable" careers unless the perception is changed. For the humanities to remain relevant in the 21st century, higher education leaders, faculty, and other stakeholders need to recognize, respect, and promote the other two career paradigms available to students and graduates: the issue-based career path and the skill-based career path. Doing so will provide a much needed approach to reality-based career advising so sorely missing on almost every campus.

Issue-Based Career Path

In addition to the knowledge-based career path, humanities majors can pursue careers related to a specific issue. Most students care deeply about one issue or another. For example, take a history major who enjoys baseball. This particular student is a woman so professional baseball is not in her future. Nevertheless, she majors in history and spends most of her undergraduate experience studying the way baseball has been perceived throughout history as new communication mediums were created. Examples of questions she studied were: what impact did television have on baseball? What impact has social media had on baseball? Luckily this particular student understood that employers seldom care about college majors so she applied for and received an internship at a local minor league baseball team. This young woman graduates cum laude with a history degree and full-time job offer from the minor league baseball team helping out with marketing and press initiatives. How is all of this possible? This humanities major understood that she could major in something that made her happy while pursuing a career related to an issue dear to her heart. She was not limited by the knowledge based career perception prevalent on most campuses. For those who might need help identifying an issue all you need to do is turn your attention toward the United Nations.

In September 2015, the United Nations (UN) General Assembly adopted the 2030 Agenda for Sustainable Development that includes 17 Sustainable Development Goals (SDGs) to transform the globe between now and 2030. The Division for Sustainable Development Goals (DSDG) in the United Nations Department of Economic and Social Affairs (UNDESA) acts as the Secretariat for the SDGs, providing substantive support and capacity-building for the goals and their related thematic issues, including water, energy, climate, oceans, urbanization, transport, science and technology, the Global Sustainable Development Report (GSDR), partnerships, and small island developing states. DSDG plays a key role in the evaluation of UN systemwide implementation of the 2030 Agenda and on advocacy and outreach activities relating to the SDGs.[18] Here is a brief listing of some of the SDGs:

1. *End poverty in all its forms everywhere.* Extreme poverty has been cut by more than half since 1990. Still, around 1 in 10 people live on less than the target figure of international-$1.90 per day.
2. *End hunger and all forms of malnutrition.* This would be accomplished by doubling agricultural productivity and incomes of small-scale food producers (especially women and indigenous peoples) by ensuring sustainable food production systems and by progressively improving land and soil quality.
3. *Ensure healthy lives and promote well-being for all at all ages.* Significant strides have been made in increasing life expectancy and reducing some of the common killers associated with child and maternal mortality. Between 2000 and 2016, the worldwide under-five mortality rate decreased by 47 percent (from 78 deaths per 1,000 live births to 41 deaths per 1,000 live births).
4. *Ensure inclusive and equitable quality education and promote lifelong learning opportunities for all.* Major progress has been made in access to education, specifically at the primary school level, for both boys and girls. The number of out-of-school children has almost halved from 112 million in 1997 to 60 million in 2014. Still, at least 22 million children in 43 countries will miss out on preprimary education unless the rate of progress doubles.
5. *Achieve gender equality and empower all women and girls.* According to the UN, "gender equality is not only a fundamental human right, but a necessary foundation for a peaceful, prosperous and sustainable world." Providing women and girls with equal access to education,

[18] For more information about the UN Sustainable Development Goals visit https://sustainabledevelopment.un.org/about

health care, decent work, and representation in political and economic decision-making processes will nurture sustainable economies and benefit societies and humanity at large.

6. *Ensure availability and sustainable management of water and sanitation for all.* Worldwide, 6 out of 10 people lack safely managed sanitation services, and 3 out of 10 lack safely managed water services. Safe drinking water and hygienic toilets protect people from disease and enable societies to be more productive economically.
7. *Ensure access to affordable, reliable, sustainable, and modern energy for all.* Targets for 2030 include access to affordable and reliable energy while increasing the share of renewable energy in the global energy mix. This would involve improving energy efficiency and enhancing international cooperation to facilitate more open access to clean energy technology and more investment in clean energy infrastructure.
8. *Promote sustained, inclusive, and sustainable economic growth, full and productive employment and decent work for all.* Achieving higher productivity will require diversification and upgraded technology along with innovation, entrepreneurship, and the growth of small- and medium-sized enterprises (SMEs).
9. *Build resilient infrastructure, promote inclusive and sustainable industrialization, and foster innovation.* Mobile cellular signal coverage has improved a great deal. In previously "unconnected" areas of the globe, 85 percent of people now live in covered areas. Planetwide, 95 percent of the population is covered.
10. *Reduce income inequality within and among countries.* Sustain income growth of the bottom 40 percent of the population at a rate higher than the national average.

Can a philosophy major work for a nonprofit that has as its mission the conservation of oceans? Absolutely. Can an English major work for an organization that promotes access to technology in Third World countries? Of course. Can an anthropology major work for a market research firm? Without a doubt. Multiple opportunities exist for humanities majors willing to consider the issue-based career path. Students should feel free to major in whatever makes them happy. My second book *Major in Happiness: Debunking the College Major Fallacies* discusses this in greater detail. This paradigm shift will be difficult, however, for students who are not exposed to this type of thinking. When humanities majors find an issue based job professors often discount it as a failure since the graduate was unable to land a knowledge based job. The knowledge based career path is so ingrained across college campuses any employment outside of it is perceived as tantamount to treason. How dare a history major have a career with a baseball team!

For those who would like more information on how to find jobs at nonprofit organizations that support one or more of the 17 SDGs, or perhaps other relevant issues, use www.encore.org or www.idealist.org. Encore is the most comprehensive site for anyone interested in starting an encore career. Its Job Listings page includes a link to Encore Career Finder, a service that "scours more than 5 million listings for encore-friendly jobs" and lets you search by field and location. Also included are links to other nonprofit job boards, plus helpful videos and articles about searching for nonprofit work. Idealist.org is a nonprofit clearinghouse. Its robust jobs board recently featured roughly 10,000 jobs as well as a database of nearly 80,000 nonprofits.

The Skill-Based Career Path

In addition to the knowledge- and issue-based career paths, there is a third option available for a humanities major to remain relevant to the twenty-first century workplace: the skill-based career path. Let's go back to that history major example from the last section. Using the skill-based career paradigm, perhaps this young woman enjoys telling stories. After all, she is a history major and telling stories is critical component of her undergraduate experience! As an undergraduate she has had to make several written and oral presentations tracing a story from the beginning to its logical conclusion. She has had to assess sources, create a chronology, and present her information in a clear, concise, and compelling manner. She truly loves studying history. But she also loves baseball. Armed with the knowledge that an internship will help her grow both professionally and personally, she applies for and receives an internship at a local baseball team. During the interview she discusses her love of storytelling yet manages to exclude any mention of the "holy trinity" of where she is going to college, her major, or her GPA. Using this skill-based career paradigm she is well aware that there is little correlation between the "holy trinity" and future income potential. The manager of the team is conducting the interview. Prior to the interview he received news that his sports information director left. Since he has a need to fill the manager mentions this to the student. She realizes that her skill of story-telling, when coupled with her love of baseball, will help her learn the role of a sports information intern. The student ensured the manager that she was a quick study (another skill) and would be honored to be their intern as long as they allowed her time to learn on the job. She accepted the job and learned first-hand what a sports information director does. They tell stories! The baseball team needed someone who could tell stories and understood the game. She utilized her skill for a career she did not even know existed. For humanities majors willing to look outside of the typical knowledge-based career paradigm, the skill-based paradigm opens an entirely new world of possibilities.

What are some other skills employers are looking for today? In no particular order, here are the top 15 skills most employers will identify as critical to the success of someone launching a career. Humanities majors take heed, all of these are within your grasp and, hopefully, your experiential learning opportunities provided opportunities for you to develop one or more of these skills. Interestingly enough, most of these also appear on the list of skills that more experienced professionals need to work on if they would like to obtain leadership and managerial positions.

1. *Empathy*: Critical to building trust and connecting with people. Slow down and learn to find out how people are feeling. Get to know your colleagues, but don't be so intrusive as to come off as offensive. Realize that everyone has struggles. Also understand that most people have created barriers to survive so use rely on empathy to make a connection.
2. *Ability to influence peers*: Work is not just about work. Work is about working with people who are in different departments, have other agendas, and want to focus on something else. Thus, it is important to have the ability to influence colleagues, even if you do not have direct authority over them, to accomplish a specific task.

3. *Emotional intelligence*: Also known as EQ. The ability to assess and manage your own emotions as well as build meaningful professional relationships is one of the most important skills successful leaders possess.
4. *Curiosity and positivity*: If you demonstrate both curiosity and positivity, you will go a long way in differentiating yourself from others in the workplace. Humanities majors are generally curious since they have studied subjects that rely on curiosity as part of the learning process. And if you are positive you will be easy to work with; a trait found far too seldom on the modern workplace.
5. *Active listening*: When someone is speaking to you look away from whatever screen is in front of you and make eye contact. Active listening means focusing on the person in front of you and ensuring they understand you heard what they said.
6. *Humility*: Humanities majors that want to succeed in the workplace need to balance a firm belief in their work with the humility to ask others for input. Doing so will help you build relationships since people like to be included in the decision-making process.
7. *Oral and written communication skills*: Time and again employers highlight oral and written communication skills as the number one trait lacking in recent college graduates.
8. *Creative problem-solving*: Humanities majors would serve themselves well by remembering the STAR method when discussing their ability to solve programs. STAR involves discussing the specific situation, task, action, and result of a situation. Doing so effectively will help people understand how you are a creative problem-solver.
9. *Resilience*: The old adage "fall down seven times; get up eight" is a useful tool for humanities majors as they launch their career. Practicing grit, or perseverance, will help recent graduates see the value of working through difficult situations and gleaning learning from each one.
10. *Observation skills*: Learning to observe, and see beyond the obvious, is paramount to achieving any long-term success. Practice observing what is said compared to what is not said as well as how people interact in meetings.

11. *Ability to contextualize*: There is always a bigger picture within an organization and often times entry level workers fail to contextualize situations. Humanities majors are usually good at seeing the big picture and then working through how specific situations fit into that. Doing so will go a long way in helping humanities majors maintain their relevance.
12. *Willingness to ask questions*: There is nothing wrong with asking questions, especially of those who have worked on a similar project. Asking questions is a strength and not a weakness. Better to ask than to do it wrong in the first place and then need to redo the work.
13. *Courage to make recommendations*: No matter how junior the role, learn to make recommendations to your leader and team with justification for your recommendation. Accept that they may not take your recommendation, yet be brave in offering your opinion on next steps and decisions rather than looking to others to tell you what to do. Doing so will show your commitment and courage to be a problem-solver and solution seeker.
14. *Relationship building*: Working with people who are different from you is often overlooked as a critical skill. Most organizations today have a dynamic workforce so it is likely that your colleagues will not look or sound like you. Learn to build relationships with everyone.
15. *Self-awareness*: Professional development is directly linked to personal growth. Therefore, if you want to develop as a professional, you will need to grow as a person. Self-awareness is perhaps the most critical skill humanities majors can work on as they look for ways to maintain relevance to the twenty-first century workplace.

As Stephanie Scorziello of *USA Today* noted regarding humanities majors,

> If you're coming into any organization, it's absolutely critical that you do think critically. Unless you're super specialized, you're probably not coming in with a lot of hard skill value. So your value is going to come from how you're going to benefit the organization in more of a soft skill way. It's super important

> to ask questions, think critically, and collaborate. You can't be afraid. You have to be willing to ask questions and work with people.[19]

Let's turn our attention to one example of a skill-based job that a humanities major could apply to.

Example of a Skill-Based Job: Nonprofit Fundraising Development—Entry Level

We are seeking applicants who will work closely with our client base. We are looking to train across events, sales, and client management. Our office needs enthusiastic candidates to assist in the development and implementation of our strategic plans. Responsibilities include:

- Executing marketing, sales, public relations, promotion and communications campaigns
- Increase customer acquisition and retention
- Implementation of product launches
- Collaborating on development of marketing and communications strategy

Job Requirements:

- Must possess strong and creative communication (oral and written), and customer service skills.
- Must demonstrate flexibility, initiative, ability to prioritize, strong organizational skills, and ability to manage deadlines in a fast paced environment.
- Must be comfortable networking in-person.
- Strong initiative, creativity, and attention to detail.

---

[19] 2019. *Humanities and Social Science Majors Please Apply: Focusing on Liberal Arts Helps Students Get Jobs.* Pearson.

- Requires flexible hours (some early mornings, late evenings, or weekends) and a willingness to travel to participate in events.

Here is a position entirely based on skills: communication, flexibility, networking, and attention to detail. If a humanities major is interested in this job, they should follow the directions on how to create a clear, concise, and compelling story as outlined in Chapter 3. Remember, humanities majors are relevant to the twenty-first century workplace and need to keep an open mind as there are many opportunities when traveling the three career paths of knowledge, issues, and skills. It would be helpful, however, if higher education institutions endorsed this three-career-path approach in order for humanities majors to maintain relevance in the twenty-first century workplace.

Jobs Outside of Academy

Just as undergraduate humanities majors need to rethink career opportunities and expand their horizons by including issue-based and skill-based job opportunities, so too do graduate students. The National Science Foundation has found that doctoral graduates in science, math and engineering degrees fields are struggling to find work as PhDs have a less than 50 percent chance of having a full-time job, and that percentage has been decreasing for about 20 years.[20] "Worse yet, as of 2011, approximately one-third of people graduating with a doctoral degree in science, technology, math or engineering had no job or postdoctoral offer of any kind." [21] Since most graduate students hyper-focus in one specific aspect of the knowledge career path, these numbers come as no surprise. By limiting the number of career opportunities those enrolled in a humanities graduate program do themselves a grave disservice. One needs to look no further than the fact that "a quarter of the families of part-time college

---

[20] 2013. "Are There Too Many Ph.Ds and Not Enough Jobs?" *NPR*, March 10.

[21] 2013. "Are There Too Many Ph.Ds and Not Enough Jobs?" *NPR*, March 10.

faculty members are on public assistance."[22] This job crisis, or lack of ability to think differently about the issue or skill-based career paths "may be just the impetus graduate humanities education needs in order to recognize that what it has to offer is essential to training leaders in a whole range of fields, far beyond academics."[23]

But higher education institutions have done little to help society at large understand the application of a liberal arts education to "fields far beyond academics." Since many professors lack such experience beyond education, it is often difficult for them to help students understand the enormous potential and various employment possibilities that exist for liberal arts majors. "Students should not have to find those careers on their own," argues Krebs and they certainly should not be disparaged for taking employment positions outside of academia, especially since academia holds little promise for future employment for most graduates.[24]

Instead of seeing liberal arts majors as being trained for one narrow career path, higher education institutions need to think differently. Far too often schools focus on how students can use the "furniture or specific body of knowledge" to find a job. Instead, colleges should consider doing much more to help students understand that the "discipline" of mind—the ability to adapt to constantly changing circumstances, confront new facts, and find creative ways to solve problems is far more applicable when looking for employment. As one music major noted,

> As a performing musician, one advantage I have is that it's possible to be professionally active without being in academe. Many musicians pursue careers in orchestras or opera houses, or prefer

[22] Jacobs, K., I. Perry, and J. MacGillvary. April 2015. "The High Public Cost of Low Wages Poverty-Level Wages Cost U.S. Taxpayers $152.8 Billion Each Year in Public Support for Working Families." University of California at Berkeley Center for Labor Research and Education. Also see Patricia, C. 2015. "Working, But Needing Public Assistance Anyway." *The New York Times*, April 12.

[23] Paula, K. 2010. "A New Humanities Ph.D." *Inside Higher Ed*, May 24.

[24] Paula, K. 2010. "A New Humanities Ph.D." *Inside Higher Ed*, May 24.

to freelance in major cities. A faculty job teaching music is by no means the universal career goal in my field.[25]

A teaching job is in fact no means the universal career goal for most students who major in liberal arts. Students majoring in history, English, philosophy, and other liberal arts need to realize that they have a tremendously valuable skill set, a discipline of the mind that is applicable to so many different industries.

Commenting on the potential, if not absolute necessity, for liberal arts majors to find employment beyond education, Richard A. Greenwald, dean of the Caspersen School of Graduate Studies and a professor of history at Drew University, observed that humanities professors "too often overvalue a mirror image of themselves and it is sad and terribly wrong when graduate programs highlight graduates who received tenure-track placements and ignore its alumni teaching at community colleges or working in museums—or, God forbid, in business or government."[26] According to Greenwald, "We need to find a way to recognize more than one successful outcome for graduate education. Our job is to train smart, able people to contribute to the intellectual and cultural life of the nation, and we have failed."[27]

Such hubris and admiration of all things similar limits progress, demeans education, and narrows the vision required for higher education institutions to create novel strategies to help students deal with and adapt to the hyper-change and dynamic global marketplace of the twenty-first century. What is more, thinking that life outside of the academy cannot exist, or even flourish, for liberal arts majors in "God forbid business or government" also demonstrates time and again that practitioners lack the ability to necessary training and experience to help their students understand the realm of what is possible.

---

[25] Lauren, B. 2004. "Coming Home to Teach." *The Chronicle of Higher Education*, November 11.

[26] Greenwald, R. 2010. "Graduate Education in the Humanities Faces A Crisis. Let's Not Waste It." *The Chronicle of Higher Education*, April 9.

[27] Greenwald, R. 2010. "Graduate Education in the Humanities Faces A Crisis. Let's Not Waste It." *The Chronicle of Higher Education*, April 9.

Conclusion

Higher education institutions need to address the perception disconnect and help the humanities maintain their relevance in the twenty-first century workplace. Doing so requires faculty to recognize and teach the three career paths available to all college students and graduates: knowledge-, skill-, and issue-based. In order for humanities majors to remain relevant in the twenty-first century workplace they need to constantly remind themselves of these three available career paths. Moreover, humanities students and graduates need to understand that one's undergraduate or graduate major is often a secondary or tertiary aspect of employment consideration. Employers understand that one's willingness to work with others, skill set, and dedication to the mission of an organization, remain far more important than where someone graduated, their GPA, or their academic major.

A study by the Brookings Institution analyzed the market value of the twenty-five most commonly cited skills listed by alumni of each college in their LinkedIn profiles. It demonstrated that skill development, not your undergraduate major or the college you choose, is most critical to your earnings potential.[28] Recognizing that many employers are unhappy or disengaged from their work, one observer noted "It's no wonder many of us aren't fully satisfied with where we're at professionally. We keep ignoring that crucial personal component that helps drive great results."[29] It is time that higher education institutions pay attention to that crucial personal component of a student's undergraduate experience. To develop that crucial personal component, and to succeed in the job market of today and tomorrow, workers across all industries and titles will need to engage in a great deal of self-reflection. Doing so will allow people to get better at the skills of human interaction. As Geoff Colvin noted in *Humans Are Underrated: What High Achievers Know that Brilliant Machines Never Will*, workers need to "become champions

---

[28] Rothwell, J., and S. Kulharni. April 2015. "Beyond College Rankings: A Value-Added Approach to Assessing Two and Four-Year Schools." *Brookings.*

[29] Bowen, J.T. 2015. "The Link Between Personal Development and Professional Success." *Huffington Post*, March 4.

at the skills of human interaction—empathy above all, social sensitivity, collaboration, storytelling, solving problems together, and building relationships."[30] Once higher education institutions address the perception disconnect, they can then turn their attention toward the vocation disconnect. Doing so will help the humanities remain relevant in the twenty-first century workplace by illustrating the dynamics required to launch and sustain a career.

---

[30] Colvin, G. 2015. *Humans Are Underrated: What High Achievers Know that Brilliant Machines Never Will.* New York, NY: Portfolio Press.

CHAPTER 5

The Vocation Disconnect

> If you say that getting the money is the most important thing, you'll spend your life completely wasting your time. You'll be doing things you don't like doing in order to go on living, that is to go on doing thing you don't like doing, which is stupid.[1]
>
> —Alan Watts

Introduction

The lack of support to help humanities majors understand what is involved in terms of skills, knowledge, and experiences to launch a career and find a vocation in today's dynamic global marketplace marks the next disconnect. Helping humanities majors comprehend how to launch a career or develop a vocation often takes a back seat to the holy trinity of institutional success: recruitment, retention, and graduation. These three drivers of enrollment, finance, and accreditation remain so important that the institution often ignores teaching humanities majors about the dynamics involved with vocational development in the 21st century. This vocation disconnect is critical to address since students tend to agonize about their choice of major, but it turns out that for many, it simply is irrelevant.

Many college graduates never work in the field related to their academic major. In one study, 47 percent of college graduates did not find a first job that was related to their college major while 32 percent said that

[1] Watts, A. 2019. "What If Money Was No Objective." https://genius.com/Alan-watts-what-if-money-was-no-object-annotated (accessed May 23, 2019).

they had never worked in a field related to their majors.[2] Every student, regardless of major, needs to understand that your college major does not determine your career.[3] Higher education institutions, however, seldom help students understand this fact. As professor Peter Cappelli of The Wharton School at the University of Pennsylvania observed, "it seems that what a person studies in college should relate to his or her planned career path, but it turns out that it's very hard to predict how those two things will interact with each other."[4] Employers have shifted their attention away from focusing on a graduate's major to a candidate's soft skills.[5] Getting boards, presidents, senior executives, and faculty to think and act differently, however, remains a challenging proposition for even the most progressive of campuses. Most academic departments still exist as silos. But such a system is antiquated. As author Ryan Craig wrote, "university units are dinosaurs that are fast becoming extinct. By getting rid of organizational silos and focusing on how to best serve students—from applicants' first interactions through decades as alumni—students win and universities win."[6] Perhaps nowhere is a win more necessary than in helping humanities majors learn about the skills, experiences, and knowledge required to launch and sustain a career in the 21st century.

---

[2] O'Shaughnessy, L. 2013. "New Study Shows Careers and College Majors Often Don't Match." *CBS News*, November 15, https://cbsnews.com/news/new-study-shows-careers-and-college-majors-often-dont-match/ (accessed April 28, 2019)

[3] Koenig, R. 2018. "Your College Major Does Not Define Your Career." *U.S. News & World Report*, September 24, 2018. https://money.usnews.com/careers/applying-for-a-job/articles/2018-09-24/your-college-major-does-not-define-your-career (accessed April 17, 2019).

[4] Lam, B. 2015. "The Danger of Picking a Major Based on Where the Jobs Are." *The Atlantic*, June 12.

[5] Koenig, R. 2018. "Your College Major Does Not Define Your Career." *U.S. News & World Report*, September 24. https://money.usnews.com/careers/applying-for-a-job/articles/2018-09-24/your-college-major-does-not-define-your-career (accessed April 17, 2019).

[6] Craig, R. 2017. "College Silos Must Die For Students To Thrive." *Forbes*, April 14, https://forbes.com/sites/ryancraig/2017/04/14/college-silos-must-die-for-students-to-thrive/#5d98c9d6222d

Explaining the Disconnect

The majority of students entering college this decade will have future jobs that will require graduates to be adept at working in diverse settings and to have the ability to relate both to machines and to other people. "Future jobs will require people to solve complex problems for which there may be no simple solutions as well as the ability to work with new information—acquiring it, assessing its value, and communicating it to others."[7] The 21st century workplace increasingly demands those skills and higher education institutions need to adapt in order to help humanities majors maintain their relevance to the 21st century workplace. Such a process will require colleges to admit that the nature of work continues to evolve and they must make a commitment to change in order to prepare all students for a volatile, uncertain, complex, and ambiguous (VUCA) future.[8] This commitment to change also involves a recognition of the three main reasons behind the vocation disconnect. First, most curricula are outdated. Second, career services offices are often ignored, underutilized, or lacking institutional support. And finally, there is little support to include career planning in the curriculum.

Problem-solving, the ability to connect different aspects of business, to think in a holistic way and the courage to deal with uncertainty and ambiguity are often cited as critical skills employers are looking for today. Therefore, universities in general, and business schools specifically, need to develop curricula that satisfy the needs of employers who require a workforce that can evolve alongside a continuously changing world. Since schools continue to teach subjects in silos, as if there is no connection or overlap between them in the real world, this vocation disconnect continues to exist.

---

[7] Humphreys, D. 2018. "Life's Different for Today's Students—Let's Help them Succeed with High Quality Learning." *Medium*, March 5, https://medium.com/todays-students-tomorrow-s-talent/lifes-different-for-today-s-students-and-for-us-if-we-re-going-to-help-them-succeed-658bdb290ca6 (accessed May 21, 2019).

[8] Humphreys, D. 2018. "Life's Different for Today's Students—Let's Help them Succeed with High Quality Learning." *Medium*, March 5, https://medium.com/todays-students-tomorrow-s-talent/lifes-different-for-today-s-students-and-for-us-if-we-re-going-to-help-them-succeed-658bdb290ca6 (accessed May 21, 2019).

> The outcome of this is that business education has become more akin to a factory line than the broad learning opportunity it should be. After all, business is a social phenomenon. It makes little sense to look at business in a vacuum, as if social science subjects such as politics and sociology do not matter, let alone teaching business as if each discipline were discrete items.[9]

Helping humanities majors understand the value their specific discipline has in the world outside of the academy remains a critical issue that must be addressed. Liberal arts professors who are uninterested in making their instruction more practical are simply out of touch. "Over 80 percent of freshman go to college to get a career and a good professor wants to meet their students where they are," she said. [10] It's hard for children to see how their dissected education will help them in the real world. There are no jobs called "math" or "Spanish." It's up to educators to help them to understand what part each of these individual subjects could play in their futures. Teachers who have had another career are far better equipped to do this because they can list examples from their own experiences. They can tell students how these skills can be used outside of an educational setting where the majority of children will end up working as adults.[11] If faculty are unwilling to help humanities majors understand how to remain relevant in the 21st century workplace, career services offices should do so.

Education leaders ought not to think of the student as the only customer of their work. In some ways, employer partners are just as important in identifying ways in which postsecondary training can lead to a good

---

[9] Tse, T., and M. Esposito. 2014. "Academia is Disconnected from the Real World." *Financial Times*, March 30, https://ft.com/content/4f5fc7a2-7861-11e3-831c-00144feabdc0 (accessed April 17, 2019).

[10] Fadulu, L. 2018. "Why Aren't College Students Using Career Services?" *The Atlantic*, January 20, 2018, https://theatlantic.com/education/archive/2018/01/why-arent-college-students-using-career-services/551051/ (accessed April 17, 2019).

[11] Brunskill, A. 2018. "The Best Teachers Have Real World Experience." *Education*, December 2018, https://education.media/the-best-teachers-have-real-world-experience-opinion (accessed April 17, 2019).

job. Just last year, Gallup found that though about half of U.S. college graduates report visiting the career services office at least once during their undergraduate experience, they are equally likely to say their experience was "not at all helpful" (16%) as they are to say it was "very helpful" (16%). Gallup and Strada reached out to students currently enrolled across 43 randomly selected colleges and universities, both public and private. The survey found that, after creating or updating a resume, students tend to use some of career centers' least beneficial services—taking a skills test, for example—more than they do the more beneficial ones. [12] Fewer than 20 percent of undergraduate students reach out to their school's career centers for advice on finding jobs or finding and applying to graduate programs, both of which the recent report identifies as some of a center's most valuable services. Often, students instead consult with friends and family members about important decisions that can determine employment, such as choosing a major.[13]

College students' failure to fully capitalize on their career center's services in their pursuit of a job is not a new problem. But this tendency could help explain why so few students are confident they'll graduate with the skills and knowledge they need to be successful in the job market—this at a time when it's especially important for millennials to secure a comfortable income after college, as they're entering a world with fewer robust safety nets, such as social security, and skyrocketing housing prices. [14]

In his book *Skin in the Game: Hidden Asymmetries in Daily Life,* Nassim Nicholas Taleb defines the doers of society as the source of all great invention and creativity, while academia remains anchored in a protectionist fashion of their own intelligence. Taleb argues that academics

---

[12] Fadulu, L. 2018. "Why Aren't College Students Using Career Services?" *The Atlantic,* January 20, https://theatlantic.com/education/archive/2018/01/why-arent-college-students-using-career-services/551051/ (accessed April 17, 2019).

[13] Fadulu, L. 2018. "Why Aren't College Students Using Career Services?" *The Atlantic,* January 20, https://theatlantic.com/education/archive/2018/01/why-arent-college-students-using-career-services/551051/ (accessed April 17, 2019).

[14] Fadulu, L. February 2018. "Why Aren't College Students Using Career Services?" *The Atlantic,* January 20, https://theatlantic.com/education/archive/2018/01/why-arent-college-students-using-career-services/551051/ (accessed April 17, 2019).

focus their attention on winning an argument rather than winning. To help humanities win, by maintaining their relevance to the 21st century workplace, higher education administrators, faculty, and staff need to think differently and address the vocation disconnect. In order for humanities majors to maintain relevance in the 21st century workplace, institutions need to implement three specific strategies that will improve how faculty explain the various factors involved with launching a career and pursuing a vocation. First, institutions need to provide internship or apprenticeship opportunities for humanities majors. Second, colleges should incorporate the study of grit into their curriculum so humanities majors can understand this vital element involved with long-term career success. Finally, faculty should include discussions of recent evidence illustrating the different winding career paths available to college graduates. By addressing this vocation disconnect, "colleges and universities can play a role by communicating opportunities to students throughout their college careers, whether through career services, academic advising, informal advisory settings, or other institution wide resources."[15]

Internships

To address the vocation disconnect, colleges need to help humanities majors acquire an internship. NACE defines an internship as "a form of experiential learning that integrates knowledge and theory learned in the classroom with practical application and skills development in a professional setting."[16] Internships serve a variety of benefits for different students. As Nancy O'Neill wrote, "for those students just beginning to figure out their choice of major and career interests, an internship can help them to become aware of the many different kinds of organizations comprising 'the world of work,' build early professional experience, and

---

[15] Schneider, M., and M. Sigelman. 2018. *Saving the Liberal Arts: Making the Bachelor's Degree a Better Path to Labor Market Success.* American Enterprise Institute.

[16] National Association of Colleges and Employers (NACE). 2015. "Position Statement." http://naceweb.org/advocacy/position-statements/united-states-internships.aspx?intlftnav (accessed August 2, 2015).

sometimes discover what they don't want to do. For those students who are clearer about their career interests and academic pursuits, an internship can help them apply what they are learning in real world settings, gain more substantial professional experience, and begin to develop a network of people in fields that interest them."[17]

In addition to helping students transfer their classroom theory and applying to real-world scenarios, internship provides opportunities for individuals to learn how to be comfortable with ambiguity. Being able to demonstrate how one is comfortable with ambiguity, by discussing how one is both flexible and versatile for example, is among the most sought-after qualities in job candidates today. Jeff Sanders, vice chairman of CEO and board practice at executive search firm Heidrick & Struggles, said, "In the past you looked for people with a certain playbook. Now you need people with relevant experience who are adaptable and quick learners."[18] Humanities graduates who complete an internship and other experiential education opportunities often gain valuable firsthand knowledge of learning how to be comfortable with ambiguity. "Learning is enhanced when students are given the opportunity to operate outside of their own perceived comfort zones."[19] "It is essential for students' learning and growth in college to have challenging stimuli and experiences of positive restlessness because these provide the creative disequilibrium and intellectual foment that drive personal exploration and development."[20]

By providing students with opportunities to gain experience and network, internship also gives the employer a chance to assess interns as potential new hires. During the last few years, more employers are viewing internship, not the school attended or major, as the single most

---

[17] O'Neill, N. Fall 2010. "Internships as a High-Impact Practice: Some Reflections on Quality." *Peer Review*, Published by the American Association of Colleges and Universities.

[18] Fry, E., F. 2014. "9 Tips to Land Your Dream Job." *Fortune*, September 3.

[19] Chapman, S., P. McPhee, and B. Proudman. 1995. "What is Experiential Education?" In *The Theory of Experiential Education*, ed. K. Warren, 235–248. Dubuque: Kendall/Hunt Publishing Company.

[20] Dalton, J.C., and P.C. Crosby. 2008. "Challenging College Students to Learn in Campus Cultures of Comfort, Convenience and Complacency." *Journal of College and Character*, February 1.

important credential for recent graduates.[21] The results show that internships have often replaced job interviews in the selection process of a new hire. Selingo reported "40 percent of all entry-level full-time hires in the U.S. are sourced through internship programs."[22] For Facebook, Enterprise Rent-a-Car, eBay, and other leading corporations more than 70 to 80 percent of new hires come through their internship programs now, compared to about half or less just a decade ago.[23]

It is no surprise, then, to realize over 90 percent of employers think that all students, regardless of major, should graduate college having completed at least one internship.[24] Due to the hypercompetitiveness of today's global marketplace, some observers believe that completing two to three internships is imperative for recent college graduates to maintain their competitive edge.[25] "Internships are essential indicators that a student is not just a great reader and writer, but also capable of succeeding in a business environment and interacting with coworkers and clients."[26] Thus, for a growing number of college seniors that want to land employment at one of the top organizations, internships are no longer a luxury but a necessity. Recent NACE research found 61 percent of graduating seniors who completed an internship or co-op experience; among that group, nearly 57 percent of the experiences were paid, up from approximately 51 percent in 2011.[27]

---

[21] Scott, A. 2013. "What do Employers Really Want from College Grads?" *Marketplace Education*, March 4.

[22] Selingo, J.J. 2015. "Are Internships the Only Way for Recent College Grads to Grab Entry-Level Jobs?" *The Washington Post,* May 18.

[23] Selingo, J.J. 2015. "Are Internships the Only Way for Recent College Grads to Grab Entry-Level Jobs?" *The Washington Post,* May 18.

[24] Schawbel, D. 2012. "Millennial Branding Student Employment Gap Study: Companies Expect Students to have Internships But aren't Hiring Interns."

[25] Hannah, G. 2012. "The Intern Queen: Internships are no Longer Optional." February 26.

[26] Smith, J. 2012. "Internships May Be the Easiest Way to A Job in 2013." *Forbes*, December 6.

[27] 2018. "Trend is Toward Paid Internships." National Association of Colleges and Employers (NACE), Press Release Dated February 15, URL (accessed November 4, 2018).

Realize the Power of Grit

Humanities majors also need to understand that another aspect of vocation is the importance of grit. It would be extremely difficult to have a long and successful career without the ability to persevere difficult situations. Numerous researchers have concluded that getting to the corner office, long-term earnings potential, and climbing up the corporate ladder all have more to do with grit than graduating with a specific degree. Grit is by far the most important characteristic one needs to demonstrate time and again in order to translate the vision they have for their life into reality. MacArthur fellow Angela Duckworth, a psychology professor at the University of Pennsylvania, defines grit as the tendency to sustain interest in and effort toward very long-term goals and equips individuals to pursue especially challenging aims over the years and even decades. Duckworth noted that people who "accomplished great things often combined a passion for a single mission with an unswerving dedication to achieve that mission, whatever the obstacles and however long it might take."[28]

Grit is a better indicator of long-term career success than talent. No matter how talented you think you are, if you don't put in the work, it will amount to little, if any, long-term career success. In *Talent Is Overrated: What Really Separates World-Class Performers from Everyone Else,* author Geoff Colvin argues that deliberate, methodical, and sustained practice is the way to achieve true mastery. Colvin concluded that "Deliberate practice is hard. It hurts. But it works. More of it equals better performance. Tons of it equals great performance. And it is available to everyone." People with grit have a hope that's based on drive and making things happen rather than mere luck. "Grit depends on a different kind of hope," Duckworth explains in her book, *Grit: The Power of Passion and Perseverance.* "It rests on the expectation that our own efforts can improve our future. I have a feeling tomorrow will be better is different from I resolve to make tomorrow better." Unfortunately grit as a key indicator of long-term career success is seldom taught in college classrooms. This aspect of the vocation disconnect is critical to resolve if humanities majors are to

---

[28] Tough, P. 2011. "What if the Secret to Success Is Failure?" *The New York Times Magazine,* September 14.

remain relevant in the 21st century workplace. Their ability to identify, develop, and leverage grit will help humanities majors navigate the many twists and turns often involved with careers. Humanities majors need to understand that "speed bumps, obstacles, and failures are inevitable parts of the journey."[29] By embracing these as specific learning opportunities, humanities majors can strengthen their resolve and ability to succeed as they continue forward as it allows them to achieve even greater success. By focusing on the cultivation of determination, perseverance, and passion, humanities majors can help themselves navigate the many twists and turns involved with the 21st century workplace. Award-winning actor Denzel Washington provided an inspirational acceptance speech reminding people about the value of grit to navigate one's career.

Throughout history, people from all walks of life had commented on grit. In the 18th century, Benjamin Franklin noted, "Energy and persistence conquer all things." In the 20th century, President Calvin Coolidge wrote: "Nothing in this world can take the place of persistence. Talent will not. Nothing is more common than unsuccessful men with talent. Genius will not. Unrewarded genius is almost a proverb. Education will not. The world is full of educated derelicts. Persistence and determination alone are omnipotent." More recently, while accepting the 2017 NAACP Image Award for Outstanding Actor in a Motion Picture for his performance in *Fences*, Denzel Washington stated "I am particularly proud about the young filmmakers and actors coming up behind my generation, in particular Barry Jenkins. Young people understand, this young man made 10, 15, 20 short films before he got the opportunity to make *Moonlight*, so never give up. Without commitment you'll never start but more importantly without consistency you'll never finish."[30] Noting how difficult the career path was for many African American actors, Washington said, "It's not easy. If it was easy, there'd be no Kerry Washington. If it was easy, there'd be no Taraji P. Henson. If it were easy,

---

[29] Pozin, I. 2019. "How to Develop the Grit You Need to Succeed." *Inc.*, December 29. (accessed May 21, 2019).

[30] 2017. "Ease is a Greater Threat to Progress than Hardship – Denzel Washington." August 14, https://motivationmentalist.com/2017/08/14/ease-greater-threat-to-progress-than-hardship-denzel-washington/

there'd be no Octavia Spencer."[31] In conclusion, Washington proclaimed, "So, keep working. Keep striving. Never give up. Fall down seven times, get up eight. Ease is a greater threat to progress than hardship. So, keep moving, keep growing, keep learning. See you at work."[32] If humanities majors are to remain relevant in the 21st century workplace, they need to understand that "ease is a greater threat to progress than hardship."

Life Twists

Maintaining a strong sense of grit is an absolute necessity for those humanities majors and graduates who want to remain relevant in the 21st century workplace since so many people have demonstrated time and again that career paths are more winding paths than straight lines; more jungle gym than corporate ladder. Addressing the vocational disconnect involves helping humanities majors understand three of the many aspects of one's career path: changing jobs, engaging in subtle maneuvers, and recognizing that there is no one right career path. Humanities majors would serve themselves well by recalling the words of Walter Robb, co-CEO of Whole Foods Market: "Have the courage to go and do what you believe. Most people can see things, but they don't have the courage to go do it and try something." If you have the courage you can change jobs, engage in subtle maneuvers, and maintain a belief that there is no one right path to follow.

Labor Department data show that 3.4 million Americans quit their jobs in April 2018, near a 2001 peak and twice the 1.7 million who were laid off from jobs in April 2018.[33] Job-hopping is happening across industries including retail, food service, and construction, a sign of broad-based labor market dynamism. Workers have been made more confident by a strong economy and historically low unemployment, at 3.8 percent

---

[31] 2017. "Ease is a Greater Threat to Progress than Hardship – Denzel Washington." August 14, https://motivationmentalist.com/2017/08/14/ease-greater-threat-to-progress-than-hardship-denzel-washington/

[32] 2017. "Ease is a Greater Threat to Progress than Hardship – Denzel Washington." August 14, https://motivationmentalist.com/2017/08/14/ease-greater-threat-to-progress-than-hardship-denzel-washington/

[33] Harrison, D.G., and E. Morath. 2018. "In This Economy, Quitters Are Winning." *The Wall Street Journal,* July 4.

in May 2018, the lowest since 2000. In the third quarter of 2009, 2.1 percent of workers changed jobs, according to Census Bureau data. That climbed to roughly 4 percent by the first quarter of 2017, matching the highest rate since 2001.[34] Given these market dynamics, it's no surprise to learn that most people will have 12 or more jobs during their lifetime.[35] Humanities majors need to know that their first job will not be their only job; nor will it be their dream job. Changing jobs is simply part of the unfolding process of managing one's career.

Career expert Allison Chesteron believes each person is the author of their career. Ultimately, it is up to each person to carve out a satisfying career path. In a blog post Chesteron writes, "A 'dream job' sounds like a fantasy. It belies the true messiness, the yearning to wander, the serendipitous nature of what it means to author a career. The term seeks to tie all the frayed ends up in a perfect little bow, failing to acknowledge what it means to take your future into your own hands and create it from scratch. It's a fallacy. Don't let it fool you." Humanities majors need to understand that the pursuit of a dream job is a fool's errand. Real-world career advice would be to tell the humanities majors to take any job and demonstrate just how relevant they are to that specific position. After a while if they grow unsatisfied with their job, they can simply do what millions of people do each year; find a new job or engage in subtle maneuvers.

Engage in Subtle Maneuvers

The final aspect of vocational training for humanities majors involves learning about subtle maneuvers. Humanities majors and graduates need to engage in subtle maneuvers so they can purpose interests other than their day job. Seldom is such a career strategy ever discussed in college classrooms. Jon Acuff's book, *Quitter: Closing the Gap Between Your Day Job and Your Dream Job* examines the possibility and reality of translating an idea for a new product or service into a dream and not a nightmare

---

[34] Harrison, D.G., and E. Morath. 2018. "In This Economy, Quitters Are Winning." *The Wall Street Journal,* July 4.

[35] Bureau of Labor Statistics, Frequently Asked Questions, no date, (accessed May 21, 2019).

while balancing the demands of a full-time employment position. Mason Currey's book *Daily Rituals: How Artists Work* examines dozens of creative people and concludes that most of them engaged in subtle maneuvers in order to pursue meaningful creative work while also earning a living.[36] "The book makes one thing abundantly clear: There's no such thing as the way to create good work, but all greats have their way."[37] As aspiring author once wrote to Irish playwright, Oscar Wilde, asking for advice on how to have a success career as a writer. In his response, Wilde told him not to rely on earning a living from writing and declared that "the best work in literature is always done by those who do not depend on it for their daily bread."[38]

Most people would complain that they do not have enough time. As author H. Jackson Brown, Jr. said, "Don't say you don't have enough time. You have exactly the same number of hours per day that were given to Helen Keller, Pasteur, Michaelangelo, Mother Teresa, Leonardo da Vinci, Thomas Jefferson, and Albert Einstein." In *Rework*, authors Jason Fried and David Heinemeier Hansson write, "Instead of watching TV or playing a game, work on your idea. Instead of going to bed at 10, go to bed at 11. We're not talking about staying up all night or 16 hour days—we are talking about squeezing out a few extra hours a week. That's enough time to get something going. Besides, the perfect time never arrives." To remain relevant in the 21st century humanities majors will need to leverage their time and should recall the words of Franz Kafka to his finance: "Time is short, my strength is limited, the office is a horror, the apartment is noisy, and if a pleasant, straightforward life is not possible, then one must try to wriggle through by subtle maneuvers."[39] During the day, Kafka worked his *brotberuf*, literally "bread job," a job done only to pay the bills, at an insurance company and then he would pursue his

---

[36] Currey, M. 2013. *Daily Rituals: How Artists Work,* Knopf.

[37] Wilwol, J. 2013. "Daily Rituals,' of the Brilliantly Creative." *NPR Books,* April 30.

[38] Khomami, N. 2013. "Literary Success? Don't Give up the Day Job, Advised Oscar Wilde." *The Telegraph,* March 19.

[39] Currey, M. 2013. *Daily Rituals: How Artists Work,* 83. Alfred A. Knopf.

passion of writing at night and during the weekend. This subtle maneuver approach has been utilized by many successful people.

Examples of those who engaged in subtle maneuvers include Joseph Heller who thrived in magazine advertising by day and wrote *Catch-22* in the evenings, sitting at the kitchen table in his Manhattan apartment. According to Heller, "I spent two or three hours a night on it for eight years...I gave up once and started watching television with my wife. Television drove me back to *Catch-22*."[40] The American composer Charles Ives never let music get too far from his mind. After graduating from Yale in 1898, he secured a position in New York as a $15-a-week clerk with the Mutual Life Insurance Company.[41] Though already an accomplished and talented organist as well as composer, he was looking to create beyond the conservative musical establishment of his day. So staying in a steady job made sense. As Ives put it, if a composer "has a nice wife and some nice children, how can he let them starve on his dissonances?"[42] How did these individuals accomplish so much while working a day job? As one observer noted, "you find out a way to get more done when you're really busy. You just learn how to fit it in."[43] Humanities majors who learn to fit their subtle maneuvers in alongside a day job will realize that doing so is just one of the many career paths available to them.

Colleges have a responsibility to address the vocational disconnect to help humanities majors understand the multiple careers available to them. As Sue Shellenbarger wrote in *The Wall Street Journal*, "The old career ladders many parents climbed are gone. The number of potential occupations has more than doubled since the early 1990s, Labor Department data show. Many young adults need a longer runway just to explore their options."[44] One example of just how many options can be found in the

---

[40] Currey, M. 2013. "Daily Rituals." *Slate*, May 2.

[41] Dishman, L. 2013. "10 Famous Creative Minds That Didn't Quit Their Day Jobs." *Fast Company*, December 6.

[42] Magee, G.S. 2008. *Charles Ives Reconsidered.* University of Illinois Press.

[43] Currey, M. 2013. "Daily Rituals." *Slate*, May 2.

[44] Shellenbarger, S. 2019. "The Job Advice You Wish You Knew How to Give." *The Wall Street Journal*, May 9, https://wsj.com/articles/the-job-advice-you-wish-you-knew-how-to-give-11557135000 (accessed May 21, 2019).

10,000 PhDs Project. This University of Toronto research project found that nearly 30 percent of PhDs graduating from a physical or life sciences program between 2000 and 2015 at the University of Toronto ended up in a private sector job.[45] As a result of the many career options now available to graduates there are four common career paths people travel:

- Life Twisters make up 52 percent—those who have a distinct life path in mind but are open to occasionally veering off that path to embrace the changes life throws their way.
- Passivists form 25 percent—people who say they lack a life plan. They not only go with the flow when facing life's challenges, and take a more passive approach to its twists and turns.
- Traditionalists are 13 percent—people who say they have a plan laid out and have no intention of veering from it.
- Reinventionsists constitute 11 percent—much more proactive than life Twisters in precipitating change with the specific goal of reinventing themselves again and again.

Humanities majors need to accept the notion that their path is the right one until it's time to change. People change jobs. They change industries. People grow and develop over time. Vocational knowledge is complex and involves a variety of dynamics seldom examined on a college campus. For example, addressing the vocational disconnect also means teaching humanities majors that more Americans are redefining success and happiness in a way that doesn't involve wealth. Only around one in four Americans (27 percent) still believes that wealth determines success, according to The LifeTwist study, a survey of more than 2,000 Americans commissioned by American Express. Americans ranked their top five contributors to success, with 85 percent saying that good health is essential. Other contributors to success included finding time for the "important

---

[45] Yamimine, S. 2019. "From Textbooks to Technology: The Wonderfully Winding Path of Careers in Industry." *Medium*, April 22, 2018, https://medium.com/@samanthazy/from-textbooks-to-technology-the-wonderfully-winding-path-of-careers-in-industry-2af31d9ce7a7 (accessed May 21, 2019)

things in life" (83 percent), having a good marriage or relationship (81 percent), good management of personal finances (81 percent), having a good work–life balance (79 percent), and having a job or career you love (75 percent). But keeping an open and flexible mindset was the most universal ingredient for success: The overwhelming majority of Americans (94 percent) agree that being open to change is essential to a successful life.

Conclusion

The substantial evidence overwhelmingly demonstrates that no one college major holds a "monopoly on the ingredients for professional achievement or a life well lived."[46] As one observer succinctly noted, "it doesn't matter what you focus on, as long as you focus on it in a rigorous way."[47] In a recent survey, 93 percent of employers agreed with the statement: "a candidate's demonstrated capacity to think critically, communicate clearly, and solve complex problems is more important than their undergraduate major."[48] Contrary to what many may believe, you do not have to major in English to have a career as a writer; you do not have to study business to work as a consultant; and you do not have to study international relations or political science to get a job in government. Likewise, you are not limited to working as an archivist, librarian, or teacher as a history major. "The real world doesn't care about your degree as much as your work ethic and attitude."[49]

This type of thinking surrounding the college major needs to be advocated, explained, and supported from higher education administrators if students are to recognize the value of focusing on an academic program

---

[46] Bruni, F. 2015. "How to Survive the College Admissions Madness." *The New York Times,* March 13.

[47] Selingo, J.J. 2013. "Does the College Major Matter? Not Really." *The New York Times,* April 29.

[48] *It Takes More Than A Major: Employer Priorities for College Learning and Student Success,* An online survey among employers conducted on behalf of the Association of American Colleges and Universities by Hart Research Associates, April 10, 2013.

[49] Stahl, A. 2015. "Six Reasons Why Your College Major Doesn't Matter." *Forbes,* August 12.

they enjoy instead of what they think they should declare as a major. As one observed noted, "For years we have been focused on access, and now we need to turn our attention equally to student success. It takes courage to say we can do better."[50] For higher education institutions to improve, they will need to think and act very differently. "The current way colleges function, with their roots grounded in outdated Weberian management practices, outmoded instructional delivery systems, and archaic approaches to student and institutional support services, simply will not work for institutions that are charged with serving as major democratizing forces and economic engines for a changing population, a changing world and a rapidly evolving future."[51] Thinking differently and moving away from the usual way of doing things, however, is a formidable challenge as "people often refuse to relinquish their deep-seated beliefs even when presented with overwhelming evidence to contradict those beliefs."[52] If a higher education institution can address the vocation disconnect, it can then move on to find a way to resolve the cultivation of the self-disconnect.

---

[50] Gonzalez, J. 2012. "Community Colleges Not Up to 21st Century Mission, Their Own Report Says." *The Chronicle of Higher Education*, April 21.

[51] Riggs, J. Winter 2009. "Leadership, Change and the Future of Community Colleges." *Academic Leadership: The Online Journal* 7, no. 1, p. 22.

[52] Klapper, B. 2013. "Free Yourself from Conventional Thinking." *Harvard Business Review Blog*, May 6.

CHAPTER 6

The Cultivation Disconnect

> Someone once told me growth and comfort do not coexist. And I think it's a really good thing to remember.
>
> —Ginni Rometty

Introduction

While higher education institutions have implemented successful programs to help individuals enter and finish college, much work needs to be done in order to help students cultivate the level of self-determination required to launch and sustain a career. Self-determination theory (SDT) is a macro theory of human motivation and personality that concerns people's inherent growth tendencies and innate psychological needs.[1] The prerequisite for one to practice SDT is a sophisticated level of self-awareness that develops over time. Since SDT examines the motivation behind choices people make without external influence and interference, it stands to reason that college students, both undergraduate and graduate, with all of their career-related decisions to make, should develop a high level of self-awareness in order to engage in SDT.[2] Two of the leading SDT researchers, Edward L. Deci and Richard Ryan, have identified competence, autonomy, and relatedness as the three psychological needs essential for psychological health and well-being of an individual. To launch and navigate a career in today's hypercompetitive global marketplace, it is imperative for humanities majors to maintain ongoing self-awareness of their competence, autonomy, and relatedness in order to understand

---

[1] Wikipedia. "Self-Determination Theory." https://en.wikipedia.org/wiki/Self-determination_theory (accessed May 18, 2019).

[2] Ibid.

what motivates them. During the last two decades, however, higher education institutions have focused on providing access to college, supported retention and graduation initiatives, and engaged in what David Brooks labeled "a resume race out of control" where students focus solely on doing what it takes to land a job upon graduation.[3] Intellectual curiosity, purpose, and depth have fallen prey to the credential race. Higher education institutions now measure success as the percentage of seniors who have a job at the time of graduation, the average salary of recent graduates as well as the average salary of those who graduated 20 years earlier. To increase their marketability in today's hypercompetitive marketplace, colleges have emphasized market share over the cultivation of self-determination. As a result, "students chase success with no greater purpose to guide them. And the universities they attend, which regard them increasingly as customers rather than students, do little to provide one."[4] This cultivation disconnect remains a vital component of demonstrating the relevance of the humanities to the 21st century workplace.

Explaining the Disconnect

This cultivation disconnect is best summarized by Harvard University psychology professor Steven Pinker who noted, "Perhaps I am emblematic of everything that is wrong with elite American education, but I have no idea how to get my students to build a self or become a soul. It isn't taught in graduate school, and in the hundreds of faculty appointments and promotions I have participated in, we've never evaluated a candidate

[3] Westerberg, C.J. 2017. "Ideal Elite College Students: 'Excellent Sheep.'" *The Daily Riff,* October 12. http://thedailyriff.com/articles/ideal-elite-college-students-excellent-sheep-1202.php and David Brooks, "Becoming a Real Person." *The New York Times,* September 8, 2014. https://nytimes.com/2014/09/09/opinion/david-brooks-becoming-a-real-person.html?hp&action=click&pgtype=Homepage&module=c-column-top-span-region®ion=c-column-top-span-region&WT.nav=c-column-top-span-region&_r=0&login=email&auth=login-email (accessed May 1, 2019).

[4] Emily, E.S. 2014. "Book Review: 'Excellent Sheep: The Miseducation of the American Elite' by William Deresiewicz." *The Wall Street Journal,* August 20.

on how well he or she could accomplish it."[5] This creation of one's self in college through an ongoing process of self-awareness is paramount to the future success of any humanities major. Therefore, it is imperative that higher education institutions help liberal arts students and graduates cultivate their self in order for them to have a successful transition from college to career. As Debra Humphreys, senior vice president for academic planning and public engagement at the Association of American Colleges and Universities (AAC&U), wrote "we don't do a very good job in higher education of really intentionally helping students prepare for and make that transition from college to career."[6]

Recent evidence supports Humphreys' claim. A May 2016 study by Adecco Group, the largest professional staffing company in the world, showed 74 percent of recent college graduates felt their schools failed to fully prepare them for the professional world.[7] Amy Glaser, a senior vice president with Adecco, noted "students struggle with critical thinking, communication and other interpersonal skills and are not often given opportunities to develop their professional skills." While recent graduates may be able to use technology well, Glaser noted, "overuse can cause their verbal or written communication skills to suffer."[8] Additionally, colleges need to increase their efforts of talking to students much earlier about the role of self-awareness, what employers are expecting, and the level of engagement by employees. Discussing these three topics earlier in their college careers will avail students with opportunities for personal growth and professional development required to have a successful career launch upon graduation.

---

[5] Westerberg, C.J.2017. "Ideal Elite College Students: 'Excellent Sheep.'" *The Daily Riff*, October 12. http://thedailyriff.com/articles/ideal-elite-college-students-excellent-sheep-1202.php

[6] Musto, P. 2016. "US College Students Feel Unprepared for 'Real' World." *VOA News*, October 6. https://voanews.com/a/us-college-students-feel-unprepared-for-real-world/3539712.html (accessed April 27, 2019). https://voanews.com/a/us-college-students-feel-unprepared-for-real-world/3539712.html

[7] Musto, P. 2016. "US College Students Feel Unprepared for 'Real' World." *VOA News*, October 6. https://voanews.com/a/us-college-students-feel-unprepared-for-real-world/3539712.html (accessed April 27, 2019).

[8] Musto, P. 2016. "US College Students Feel Unprepared for 'Real' World." *VOA News*, October 6. (accessed April 27, 2019).

Self-awareness can help students make adjustments and improvements, accommodate for weaknesses, and bring into question one's identity. Without self-awareness, students subject themselves to self-deception, potentially leading some individuals to be misinformed and cause them to miscommunicate, mislearn, and misinform others.[9] Unfortunately, many students get entrenched in what Columbia University's Jack Mezirow refers to as "habits of mind" that blinds them to their own self-deception and stunts any real progress to self-awareness.[10] Colleges need to do more to help students cultivate the self-awareness required to identify one's habits of mind. "The lack of the self-awareness process in learners can create an inability to form relationships with peers, and an unrealistic view of the self is often part of the student persona."[11] Students who lack self-awareness often blame others around them for things that go wrong and block their awareness of their own responsibility for the problems they face, thus preventing solutions or progress. The inflated view that college students have of their professional skills is just one example.

Upon graduation, most recent college graduates believe their skills are polished, their experiences deep, and their readiness strong at the time of launching their career. According to the 2018 National Association of Colleges and Employers (NACE) survey, employers think otherwise. The NACE survey uncovered a stark difference in how the graduates viewed their capabilities compared to how employers found them. In almost every one of the eight categories measured, a high percentage of students indicated they were proficient. Employers disagreed. "This can be problematic because it suggests that employers see skills gaps in key areas where college students don't believe gaps exist."[12] For example, the largest divide was around students' professionalism and work ethic where 90 percent

---

[9] Steiner, P. 2014. "The Impact of the Self-Awareness Process on Learning and Leading." *New England Journal of Higher Education*, August 2014.

[10] Steiner, P. 2014. "The Impact of the Self-Awareness Process on Learning and Leading." *New England Journal of Higher Education*, August 2014.

[11] Steiner, P. 2014. "The Impact of the Self-Awareness Process on Learning and Leading." *New England Journal of Higher Education*, August 2014.

[12] Bauer-Wolf, J. 2018. "Overconfident Students, Dubious Employers." *Inside Higher Ed*, February 23, 2018. https://insidehighered.com/news/2018/02/23/study-students-believe-they-are-prepared-workplace-employers-disagree

of seniors thought they were competent but only about 43 percent of the employers agreed. Additionally, 80 percent of students believed they were competent in oral and written communication and critical thinking, while only roughly 42 percent and 56 percent of employers, respectively, indicated that students were successful in those areas.[13] If the humanities are to remain relevant to the 21st century workplace they will need to identify, explain, and develop a sense of self that forms the foundation of their career launch following graduation. To that end, higher education institutions need to implement a variety of strategies to help each humanities major and graduate develop the sense of self required of a young professional to successfully launch their career in today's volatile, uncertain, complex, and ambiguous (VUCA) world.

To address the cultivation disconnect, higher education institutions can help humanities majors and graduates increase their self-awareness in today's hypercompetitive, dynamic, and ever-changing global marketplace by implementing five strategies. First, colleges need to introduce and then explain, the five areas of well-being as students make the transition from campus to career. Second, institutions must incorporate more discussions of the relationship between self-awareness, self-discipline, and the development of one's self. Third, schools have an obligation to create programming that allows humanities majors to engage in self-determination. Fourth, colleges and universities need to include the theory and practice of positive uncertainty as part of the student experience. Finally, higher education institutions must provide lifelong learning opportunities for their humanities alumni.

Well-Being

To address the cultivation of the self-disconnect, colleges and universities need to discuss the Gallup-Sharecare Well-Being Index at both the undergraduate and graduate levels. Doing so can help humanities students better understand the complexities of well-being. In a world focused on starting

[13] Bauer-Wolf, J. 2018. "Overconfident Students, Dubious Employers." *Inside Higher Ed,* February 23, 2018. https://insidehighered.com/news/2018/02/23/study-students-believe-they-are-prepared-workplace-employers-disagree

salaries as the only thing that matters for a college graduate's happiness, students from all majors could benefit from realizing that financial compensation is merely one aspect of a much more complicated discussion on one's well-being. College students and recent graduates should also know that according to the latest data, overall well-being among U.S. adults declined substantially. In 2017 the index was 61.5, down 0.6 points from 62.1 in 2016 and on par with the lower level recorded in 2014. According to Gallup, this decline is both statistically significant and meaningfully large.[14] The Gallup-Sharecare Well-Being Index is calculated on a scale of 0 to 100, where 0 represents the lowest possible well-being and 100 represents the highest possible well-being.

The Well-Being Index consists of metrics drawn from each of the five essential elements of well-being:

- **Purpose:** liking what you do each day and being motivated to achieve your goals
- **Social:** having supportive relationships and love in your life
- **Financial:** managing your economic life to reduce stress and increase security
- **Community:** liking where you live, feeling safe and having pride in your community
- **Physical:** having good health and enough energy to get things done daily

This well-being discussion is critical since four out of five of today's college graduates want to find purpose in their work yet fewer than half say they've done so successfully.[15] Research on more experienced workers find similar results as 34 percent of U.S. employees report being engaged, 16.5 percent "actively disengaged," and the remaining 53 percent of

---

[14] Gallup Press Release. 2017. "Americans' Well-Being Declines in 2017." November 8. https://wellbeingindex.sharecare.com/americans-well-being-declines-2017/, (accessed February 2, 2018).

[15] Schwartz, N. 2019. "How one Small College Helps its Students Find 'Purposeful Work.'" *Education Dive*, April 15. https://educationdive.com/news/how-one-small-college-helps-its-students-find-purposeful-work/552695/ (accessed May 2, 2019).

workers are in the "not engaged" category. Thus, the purpose gap experienced by recent college graduates comes as no surprise.[16] The majority of American workers are simply not engaged at the workplace. Therefore, their well-being indicator is low. College students need to know that most Americans may be generally satisfied at their job but are not cognitively or emotionally connected to their work. In other words, their job pays the bills but lacks significant meaning in their lives.

This lack of engagement will confront new realities in the near future as advanced technologies introduce new ways to create value and disrupt current industries and organizational models. According to the Future of Jobs Report 2018 of the Forum's Centre for the New Economy and Society, while 75 million jobs are expected to be displaced in the next five years, another 133 million are expected to be created across 20 key developed and emerging economies.

Many other jobs that are not outright displaced will change dramatically due to automation, requiring major worker retraining and adjustment. In what should be a wakeup call to anyone teaching today, one report suggests that at least 54 percent of all employees will require reskilling and upskilling by 2022. Of these, over a third will require more than six months of additional training. However, only around 30 percent of employees in the jobs most exposed to technological disruption received any kind of training in the past year, and most companies say they intend to target retraining programs toward high-performing employees.[17] This implies that the employees most at risk of job or skill disruption are also far less likely to be provided with retraining to cope, potentially increasing inequality. If national and global actors, including multinationals as well as the education sector and policymakers, fail to support workers attaining and upgrading skills, the outcome could be a true "loselose"

---

[16] Harter, J. 2018. "Employee Engagement is on The Rise in the U.S." *Gallup*, August 26. https://news.gallup.com/poll/241649/employee-engagement-rise.aspx, (accessed August 29, 2018).

[17] World Economic Forum. April 2019. "Globalization 4.0: Shaping a New Global Architecture in the Age of the Fourth Industrial Revolution." *White Paper*, http://www3.weforum.org/docs/WEF_Globalization_4.0_Call_for_Engagement.pdf

scenario—rapid technological change accompanied by talent shortages, mass unemployment, and growing inequality. Yet that's a plausible outcome, particularly given the existing shortfall of skills essential for a tech-driven future reported by enterprises around the world.[18]

By understanding the level of engagement by workers, the well-being index, and the future necessity of learning new skills, humanities majors can go a long way in helping to manage their expectations. Far removed from the classroom managed by a liberal arts professor who has only worked in a university setting, and who most likely has the promise of a lifetime job known as tenure, the humanities graduate operating in the real world outside of the academy needs to rely on a strong sense of self. That sense of self, when coupled with a dedication to lifelong learning, will long prove the relevance of the humanities to the 21st century workplace.

Determine Your Self

To stay relevant in the 21st century workplace, humanities majors need to determine their self and then commit to a lifelong process of creating a new self. It's important to humanities graduates, as well as all graduates, to recognize the ability to create a new self. As Joan Didion wrote in *Slouching Towards Bethlehem*, "I already said goodbye to a few people I used to be."[19] If a college senior reflects upon their current self, they will soon realize their current self is different from their self as a senior in high school. Well, at least that's the hope! This constant evolution of the self is seldom discussed in university classrooms. To remain relevant in the 21st century workplace, any individual regardless of major, will need to continually reinvent themselves.

This evolutionary process of creating a new self was discussed by Hazel Rose Markus in her 1986 paper "Possible Selves." Markus's research

---

[18] World Economic Forum. April 2019. "Globalization 4.0: Shaping a New Global Architecture in the Age of the Fourth Industrial Revolution." *White Paper*, http://www3.weforum.org/docs/WEF_Globalization_4.0_Call_for_Engagement.pdf

[19] Didion, J. 1968. *Slouching Towards Bethlehem.*

redefined how psychologists think of the relationship between self and culture. In that paper she and coauthor Paula Nurius developed the concept of possible selves: the ideal self we would like to become, we could become, and we are afraid of becoming.[20]

> A person's identity involves more than the thoughts, feelings and behaviors of the current self; it also includes reflections of what a person was like in the past and hopes and fears about what a person may become in the future.[21]

Each individual has a repertoire of possible selves that serve as the "cognitive manifestation of enduring goals, aspirations, motives, fears, and threats [which] provide the essential link between the self-concept and motivation."[22] To suggest that there is a single self to which one "can be true" or an authentic self that one can know is to deny the rich network of potential that surrounds individuals and that is important in identifying and descriptive of them.[23] Possible selves contribute to the fluidity or malleability of the self because they are differentially activated by the social situation and determine the nature of the working self-concept. At the same time, the individual's hopes and fears, goals and threats, and the cognitive structures that carry them are defining features of the self-concept; these features provide some of the most compelling evidence of continuity of identity across time.

Successful people understand that they have an active role in developing who they would like to become and work hard at doing so. Such a process involves a substantial amount of experiencing, reflecting, and meaning-making throughout one's entire life. Successful people understand the value of maintaining a high level of self-awareness. They ask

---

[20] Markus, H.R., and P. Nurius. 2014. "How Many 'Selves' Do We Have?" *Being Human*, February 25.

[21] Dunkel, C., and J. Kerpelman, ed. 2006. *Possible Selves: Theory, Research and Applications*, New York, NY: Nova Science Publishers, Inc.

[22] Markus, H.R., and P. Nurius. 2014. "How Many 'Selves' Do We Have?" *Being Human*, February 25.

[23] Ibid.

themselves important questions and keep doing so throughout their life. One of the most important questions successful people ask themselves is, "Why am I doing what I am doing?" Humanities majors who engage in such self-reflection, and then leverage lessons learned, will serve themselves well as they look to engage in self-determination and remain relevant in the 21st century workplace.

Engage in Self-Determination

Successful people learn how to engage in self-determination. Self-determination theory (SDT) is an approach to human motivation and personality that articulates enhanced performance, persistence, and creativity, arguably the three critical skills everyone needs to succeed, best fostered by an individual developing a sense of autonomy, competence, and relatedness.[24] These three traits—autonomy, competence, and relatedness—are characteristics often found in successful people. Co-developed by two University of Rochester psychology professors, Edward L. Deci and Richard M. Ryan, SDT "focuses on the social-contextual conditions that facilitate versus forestall the natural processes of self-motivation and healthy psychological development."[25]

Part of self-determination is experiencing failure, disappointment, and discomfort and learning how to work through each situation. Unfortunately, helicopter or snowplowing parents shield their children from even the slightest degree of discomfort. Failure is a distant shore that children of intrusive parents seldom see. Children are sometimes home-schooled to prevent them from being exposed to people, ideas, and material the parents deem inappropriate. Prohibiting children from people or ideas you deem uncomfortable for your child to process and then expecting them to mature into well-adjusted, autonomous adults able to connect

---

[24] Self-determination Theory website: www.selfdeterminationtheory.org/theory/ (accessed August 6, 2015).

[25] Ryan, R.M., and Deci, E.L. 2000. "Self-Determination Theory and the Facilitation of Intrinsic Motivation, Social Development, and Well-Being." *American Psychologist* 55, pp. 68–78.

with others is simply unrealistic.[26] As one mother said, "We need to let our kids chart their own course and make their own mistakes."[27] Competence is one of the three foundational elements of self-determination, but children need to learn that they can't be good at everything. To learn lessons of failure, disappointment, or discomfort, children need to experience those things as early as elementary school. Such lessons should be reinforced since high school students, college students, and young professionals need to experience disequilibrium but at greater levels. Doing so can equip them with the skills necessary to deal with life's issues throughout adulthood. The experience of psychological and cognitive disequilibrium produces feelings of internal "dissonance" that manifests itself as uncertainty, and sometimes as conflict and even threat. [28]

> But it is the experience of such dissonance that opens up the possibility for learning and growth because it nudges students into confronting and considering new ways of understanding, thinking, and acting that help to unsettle the old and integrate it with the new.[29]

UCLA psychiatrist Paul Bohn_believes many parents will do anything to avoid having their child experience even mild discomfort, anxiety, or disappointment.[30] Shielding a child from psychological and cognitive disequilibrium, failure, or discomfort provides a tremendous disservice; "with the result that when, as adults, they experience the normal frustrations of life, they think something must be terribly wrong."[31] "It is essential for students' learning and growth in college to have challeng-

---

[26] Wallace, K. 2014. "Longing for the Carefree Parenting Style of Yesterday?" *CNN News*, August 25.
[27] Ibid.
[28] Jon Dalton, J., and Pamela P. Crosby, . 2008. "Challenging College Students to Learn in Campus Cultures of Comfort, Convenience and Complacency," *Journal of College and Character* 9, no. 3, pp. 1–5.
[29] Ibid.
[30] Kampakis, K.K. 2014. "10 Common Mistakes Parents Today Make." *Huffington Post*, March 3.
[31] Ibid.

ing stimuli and experiences of positive restlessness because these provide the creative disequilibrium and intellectual foment that drive personal exploration and development."[32] To engage in self-determination in today's volatile, uncertain, complex, and ambiguous (VUCA) global marketplace, humanities majors and graduates will also need to practice the paradoxical principles of positive uncertainty.

Positive Uncertainty

Instead of telling students that all they need is the right college majors at the right institution with the right grade point average (GPA) in order to land their dream job, presidents, boards, and faculty should instead help students understand positive uncertainty. Since success has little, if any, correlation to one's college, major, or GPA, humanities majors and graduates need to know that the path before them is filled with unforeseen questions, issues, and problems. How one navigates the chaos of launching and sustaining a career depends upon their ability to remain positive amidst the ambiguity. Unfortunately, most institutions market their majors as the right ones leading to amazing careers with exorbitant salaries. This does little to help the majority of humanities majors who are searching for ways to navigate the many issues along the way of launching their career. Institutions would serve humanities majors and graduates a great service by discussing the tenants of positive uncertainty.

Researcher H. B. Gelatt and Carol Gelatt developed four factors—want, know, believe, and do—into four paradoxical principles. These four principles are paradoxical because they are contradictory statements that may nevertheless be true. Each principle embraces conventional decision-making wisdom and contradicts it. It's not an either-or approach to decision making but a both-and-more.[33] Humanities majors who understand and practice positive uncertainty can maintain the flexibility of mind, the determination of spirit, and the necessity of perspec-

---

[32] Dalton, J., and P. Crosby. 2008. "Challenging College Students to Learn in Campus Cultures of Comfort, Convenience and Complacency." *Journal of College and Character* 9, no. 3, pp. 1–5.

[33] http://gelattpartners.com/positiveuncertainty.html

tive required to land employment opportunities some might consider unconventional.

Be focused and flexible about what you want: Traditional decision theory stresses being focused on your future goals. This strategy is not obsolete but incomplete. Being focused helps you attain goals. It keeps you from getting distracted easily, but can prevent you from discovering new goals. Become flexible with what you want by asking yourself questions such as "What else could I do?," "What other possible actions are there?," or "What other choices or options for what I could do?" Being focused yet flexible reminds humanities majors to use goals as a guide and not a governing mechanism.

Be aware and wary about what you know: Information is the hallmark of decision making. When making a decision, we are told to get the facts because collecting information will reduce uncertainty. However, very often the information you have is not what you want, need, or is available. Being aware and wary about what you know helps you to assess what is known and appreciate what is unknown. The hallmark of this principle is to be open-minded where you can leverage your whole brain—the rational, factual side and the intuitive, imaginative side. Imagine a pie chart titled "knowledge" with three slices: (a) the smallest slice (10 percent) is the amount of information we know; (b) the second slice (20 percent) is the amount of information we know we don't know; and (c) the largest slice (70 percent) is the amount of information we don't know we don't know. When engaging in positive uncertainty, it's important to recognize what you do know and equally vital to be wary about what you don't know.

Be realistic and optimistic about what you believe: What you believe has always been seen as one of the most important factors in what you decide but seldom the most important factor in traditional decision-making strategies. What you believe determines what you see—and do. To be realistic is not to be totally objective. There is no such thing. Reality is not only what is "out there." It is also in the mind's eye of the beholder. The optimistic part of this principle (the nontraditional part) helps you notice how beliefs can be prophecy. Optimism leads to proactive behavior. What you believe may be the most significant factor in creative decision making. Therefore, be sure your beliefs are a bridge not a barrier when making decisions.

Be practical and magical about what you do to decide: This principle is about your decision rules, methods, and your strategy for deciding. Do you know what your decision-making strategies are? Most people don't know how they decide. To be practical and magical is to be whole brained and bodied. You use both your head and heart when deciding. Start by becoming aware of your decision strategies. Avoid rigid decision rules. Rules are for guidance not obedience. Make up your mind creatively. Every decision is different, and every strategy should be different. Become a versatile, creative decision making. What you do to decide depends on your willingness to decide. Being positive about uncertainty brings about the opportunity for proactive creativity in your decision making. If the future is certain, all you can do is prepare for it. When the future is uncertain, you have the opportunity to influence it. You can be part of the creating your future.

There is no doubt that life is uncertain. When navigating their career most people want to obtain some level of certainty that their position, department, and organization will be around for an extended period of time. This is difficult in today's economy. When navigating your career today, you need to look beyond those positions that are probable and challenge yourself to consider those that are possible. Developing a career path based on the probable will severely limit your options. Charting a career based on what is possible allows you to travel down paths previously unimagined. Acknowledge that the future involves ambiguity and paradox. Once you accept that the future is full of ambiguity and paradox, you can then realize that

> one does not know some things, cannot always see what is coming, and frequently will not be able to control it. Being positive and uncertain allows one to be able to act when one is not certain about what one is doing.[34]

Practicing positive uncertainty allows you to navigate amidst the chaos, adjust to the disruption, and live a life of intention and purpose.

---

[34] 1989. "Positive Uncertainty: A New Decision Making Framework for Counseling." *Journal of Counseling Psychology.*

As an illustration of just how uncertain the future is, one study estimated that 47 percent of the U.S. job market is at risk of being automated by 2034.[35] In less than 20 years, close to half of the jobs in America could be subjected to algorithms, robotics, or yet to be invented technologies. Entire industries are subject to change in the future. All the more reason to practice positive uncertainty as it will help you navigate such disruption.

Commit to Lifelong Learning

Higher education institutions can also help address the cultivation of the self-disconnect by providing lifelong learning opportunities for humanities majors long after graduation. Since 70 percent of today's Millennials quit their jobs within two years, there is a need for career guidance for humanities majors, as well as all graduates, during their 20's and into their 30's. It's important for institutions to recognize that their graduates require additional training throughout their life and then develop programming to support alumni when and where possible. After all, everyone is a work in progress. In their 2012 book *The Start-up of You: Adapt to the Future, Invest in Yourself, and Transform Your Career,* authors Reid Hoffman (cofounder of LinkedIn) and Ben Casnocha realize that great people, like great organizations, are in a state of perpetual growth. "They're never finished and never fully developed. Each day presents an opportunity to learn more, do more, and grow more. This state of permanent beta is a lifelong commitment to continuous personal growth."[36]

As today's dynamic global marketplace continues to present organizations with new challenges to address, problems to solve, and questions to answer, executives and human resource managers are going to need people dedicated to personal growth. Stressing the relationship between personal growth and professional success, Robert S. Kaplan, Emeritus Professor of Leadership Development at the Harvard Business School,

---

[35] Frey, C.B., and M.A. Osborne. 2013. "The Future of Employment: How Susceptible Are Jobs to Computerization?" September 17.

[36] For more information please visit *The Start Up of You* website: www.thestartupofyou.com/

observed that "fulfillment doesn't come from clearing hurdles others set for you; it comes from clearing those you set for yourself."[37] Throughout his career, Kaplan realized that ambitious professionals spend a substantial amount of time thinking about strategies that will help them achieve greater levels of success. By striving for a more impressive job title, higher compensation, or increased responsibility, ambitious professionals often allow their definition of success to be influenced by family, friends, and colleagues. Despite their achievements and high level of success, Kaplan found that many ambitious professionals lacked a true sense of professional satisfaction and fulfillment. Kaplan wrote that he met a large number of "impressive executives who expressed deep frustration with their careers. They looked back and felt that they should have achieved more or even wished that they had chosen a different career altogether."[38]

In one study of human resource directors conducted in the United Kingdom, 91 percent of respondents think that by 2018, prospective employees will be recruited on their ability to deal with change and uncertainty. Over half of the respondents said one of their key attribute for future business success is finding individuals who are able to deal with unanticipated problems.[39] In today's volatile and uncertain global economy, if you lack personal development, it may be difficult to move forward because protectionist measures from governments, companies, and unions are disappearing. Professional development is directly linked to personal growth. If you want to grow as a professional, you will need to grow as a person. *Your* specific contribution will define *your* specific benefits much more. "Just showing up will not cut it."[40] As Jacob Morgan wrote in *The Future of Work: Attract New Talent, Build Better Leaders, and Create a Competitive Organization*,

---

[37] Kaplan, R.S. July-August 2008. "Reaching Your Potential," *Harvard Business Review*.

[38] Ibid.

[39] 2015. "The Flux Report: Building a Resilient Workforce in the Face of Flux." Published by Right Management and Manpower Group, May 28.

[40] Friedman, T.L. 2013. "It's a 401(k) World." *The New York Times*, April 30.

> knowledge and experience are no longer the primary commodity. Instead, what is far more valuable is to have the ability to learn and to apply those learnings into new and unique scenarios. It's no longer about what you know, it's about how you can learn and adapt.

Higher education institutions can go a long way in helping the humanities remain relevant to the 21st century workplace by offering lifelong learning opportunities that graduates will need as they look to sustain a long-term career growth strategy in an ever-changing global marketplace.

Conclusion

In his book *Robot-Proof: Higher Education in the Age of Artificial Intelligence,* Joseph Aoun wrote that higher education should prepare students by teaching them sought-after soft skills such as creativity, ethics, and cultural agility along with technical literacy. Cathy N. Davidson's book *The New Education: How to Revolutionize the University to Prepare Students for a World in Flux* echoes Aoun's observation. Davidson suggests that higher education institutions need to support students in learning skills "that will make them not just work-force ready but world ready that include soft skills, including strategies, methods and tactics for successful communication and collaboration." Students and graduates need new ways of integrating knowledge, including by reflection on what they're learning—not more "teaching to the test." In today's volatile, uncertain, complex, and ambiguous (VUCA) global marketplace, Davidson argues that a student's greatest skill to develop is the ability to navigate a world in flux. If higher education institutions are committed to the humanities, then they should address this cultivation disconnect in order to better prepare liberal arts students and graduates to remain relevant in the 21st century workplace.

Conclusion

In October 2019 Nobel Prize winner Robert Shiller was asked about the power of storytelling as discussed in his new book *Narrative Economics.* In reflecting on the power of story as it relates to economics Shiller stated "Compartmentalization of intellectual life is bad."[1] Shiller and other "prominent economists are making the case for why it still makes a lot of sense to major (or at least take classes) in humanities alongside more technical fields."[2] In short, studying the humanities can help students maintain relevance for an ever changing 21st century global marketplace. This book provided an outline of strategies higher education institutions can use to help maintain the relevance of the humanities to the 21st century workplace.

- *Chapter 1—The Explanation Disconnect* detailed ways to help people outside of the academy understand what the humanities are.
- *Chapter 2—The Comprehension Disconnect* illustrated the need for humanities faculty, as well as presidents, boards, and other stakeholders to better comprehend the relevance of the humanities to the workplace.
- *Chapter 3—The Translation Disconnect* discussed how higher education institutions need to do a far better job helping humanities majors, as well as majors in other subjects, translate their value to the marketplace.
- *Chapter 4—The Perception Disconnect* explained how administrators, faculty, and staff need to think differently and provide humanities majors with a different perspective on different career opportunities.

---

[1] Heather, L. 2019. "The World's Top Economists Just Made the Case for Why We Still Need English Majors." *The Washington Post,* October 19, 2019.

[2] Heather, L. 2019. The World's Top Economists Just Made the Case for Why We Still Need English Majors." *The Washington Post,* October 19, 2019.

- *Chapter 5—The Vocation Disconnect* provided strategies to help faculty explain the various factors involved with launching a career and pursuing a vocation.
- *Chapter 6—The Cultivation Disconnect* highlighted the need for institutions to help humanities majors increase their self-awareness and engage in self-determination in order to prepare for life after college accordingly.

Just as students must explore new ways of mastering and certifying their command of in-demand skills, colleges must explore new methods of informing students of employer needs and potential earnings outcomes and providing active career coaching for students to maximize the value of their educational experiences.[3]

Bard College president Leon Botstein noted such in a May 24, 2019, interview published in *The Wall Street Journal* that "The humanities and the arts have made a bad case of defending themselves. On some level they've been excessively professionalized, and they've hidden behind academic language."[4] Botstein also observed: "Too many colleges simply have a curriculum that's an imitation of a graduate school—by departments. Students come with curiosity, and that curiosity doesn't fit neatly into a departmental boundary. They're interested in issues." To address that Bard has "hired so many terrific people who are not professional academics."[5]

Mark Schneider and Matthew Sigelman complimented Botstein's thoughts when they wrote in *Saving the Liberal Arts*:

---

[3] Schneider, M., and M. Sigelman. February 2018. *Saving the Liberal Arts: Making the Bachelor's Degree a Better Path to Labor Market Success.* American Enterprise Institute.

[4] Akst, D. 2019. "The Reopening of the Liberal Mind." *The Wall Street Journal,* May 24. https://wsj.com/articles/the-reopening-of-the-liberal-mind-11558732547?ns=prod/accounts-wsj (accessed May 25, 2019).

[5] Akst, D. 2019. "The Reopening of the Liberal Mind." *The Wall Street Journal,* May 24. https://wsj.com/articles/the-reopening-of-the-liberal-mind-11558732547?ns=prod/accounts-wsj (accessed May 25, 2019).

> Schools must offer more opportunities for students to build in-demand skills through strategic curriculum development, the development of work-based learning opportunities such as internships or co-ops, and stronger ties with local employers. This may be a particularly difficult challenge for colleges and universities that have tended to structure themselves around departments focused on traditional or broad-based skills.[6]

Additionally, maintaining the relevance of the humanities to the 21st century workplace will also compete with other issues that colleges need to resolve such as "bringing clarity to credentials, reckoning with racist histories and reforming remediation can help attract and retain today's students."[7] The task before higher education institutions is indeed daunting, but if the humanities are to remain relevant to the 21st century workplace, much work remains to be done.

With that in mind, let us turn our attention in this conclusion toward the work that humanities majors can do to help themselves. While higher education institutions continue to find ways to better serve their students, the number of challenges facing college administrations continues to rise. Implementing anyone of the strategies outlined in this book, regardless of cost, will most likely be a herculean task at even the most progressive of colleges. Higher education institutions are simply reluctant change no matter how much they profess otherwise. Therefore, a conclusion that details steps humanities majors can do themselves seems like a useful approach.

Since this publication provided six strategies for higher education institutions, here are six for humanities majors to use in order to remain relevant in the 21st century workplace. Even if presidents, boards, administrators, faculty, and staff implemented each of the strategies here, and every one worked perfectly, there still remains work for the humanities major to do.

---

[6] Schneider, M., and M. Sigelman. February 2018. *Saving the Liberal Arts: Making the Bachelor's Degree a Better Path to Labor Market Success.* American Enterprise Institute.

[7] Schwartz, N. 2019. "3 Changes Higher ed Leaders Should be Ready to Make." *Education Drive,* May 13. https://educationdive.com/news/3-changes-higher-ed-leaders-should-be-ready-to-make/554594/

- *Self-Reliance*: Humanities majors should commit to a high level of self-reliance. With the rise of helicopter parents, young professionals lack the level of self-reliance required to navigate the chaos of today's volatile, uncertain, complex, and ambiguous global marketplace. The job of any parent is to ensure that their child can live without them. Stop relying on others and start making your way in the world through an ability to demonstrate competence, a compelling display of autonomy, and an unmatched level of relating to others. Danish philosopher Søren Kierkegaard noted: "A man who as a physical being is always turned toward the outside, thinking that his happiness lies outside him, finally turns inward and discovers that the source is within him." Happiness is indeed a choice. We choose to be happy. But we also choose to identify the source of our happiness. When we want to be happy, we look for strong positive emotions like joy, enthusiasm, and excitement. Unfortunately, research shows that this isn't the best path to happiness. According to multiple studies, the more value people placed on happiness, the less happy they became. For example, research led by the psychologist Ed Diener reveals that happiness is driven by the frequency, not the intensity, of positive emotions. When we aim for intense positive emotions, we evaluate our experiences against a higher standard, which makes it easier to be disappointed. If you want to experience joy or meaning, you need to, as Kierkegaard suggested, look inward in order to shift your attention away from happiness and toward projects and relationships that bring joy and meaning as byproducts.
- *Discover Leisure*: Engage in something merely because you enjoy it. As author K. J. Dell'Antonia wrote in *The New York Times*, "The opportunities are there, but the will to take advantage of them, to make choices for reasons other than profit or productivity, has to be yours." Whether you are a freshman who just declared a humanities major or a graduate five years removed from commencement, realize the value of engaging in something merely because you enjoy it in order

to listen to yourself.[8] If you want to be relevant to the 21st century workplace, select a major that makes you happy and engage in leisure activities that allow you to develop your current self into a future self that is autonomous, creative, and collaborative—three skills that will remain important for employers across all industries in the future.

- *Run the Numbers*: Before you commit to any college know the numbers. Take the time to really understand your financial aid package. Grants generally do not need to be paid back. Loans have to be. How much will your out of pocket costs be? How much will your parents have to contribute? Figure that out for one year and then multiply by four. Can you afford to be that much in debt at the age of 22? Do your parents have the cash required or do they have to borrow money? Can they afford to do so? The 2018 report *Decoding the Cost of College: The Case for Transparent Financial Aid Award Letters* reviewed 11,000 financial award letters and found confusing jargon and terminology, omission of the complete cost, vague definitions, and inconsistent bottom line calculations as just some of the key findings.[9] If you want to be relevant to the 21st century workplace, have an understanding of your own finances. Doing so will help you become financially literate. You can be a humanities major and graduate with very little debt if you are savvy about analyzing how much college will cost you.
- *Best v. Right*: Successful people spend a good deal of time comparing their best option to the right one. This is an important stepping stone to use as people will often be blinded by the allure of the "best" of something instead of the "right" one. This is often the case with the selection of what

[8] Dell'Antonia, K.J. 2019. "How High School Ruined Leisure." *The New York Times,* May 18. (accessed May 20, 2019).

[9] Burd, S., R. Fishman, L. Keane, J. Habbert, B. Barrett, K. Dancy, S. Nguyen, and B. Williams. 2018. *Decoding the Cost of College: The Case for Transparent Financial Aid Award Letters,* June 5. (accessed May 1, 2019).

college to attend, major to select, or company to work for. People believe that they need to go to the best school. The best school provides the best education and the best opportunities to get the best job for the best career to have the best life. Nothing could be further from the truth. Successful people know that identifying the right option, not the best one, is the stepping stone. The latest research regarding this topic can be found in Malcolm Gladwell's book *David and Goliath: Underdogs, Misfits, and The Art of Battling Giants*, who observed: "We strive for the best and attach great importance to getting into the finest institutions we can. But rarely do we stop and consider whether the most prestigious of institutions is always in our best interest." That type of thinking can be applied to almost anything in life. When making a decision, are you focused on the best option or the right one? As Coach Herb Brooks said when building the 1980 U.S. Olympic hockey team: "I'm not looking for the best players. I'm looking for the right ones." Selecting the right players allowed Brooks to build a team that would go on and upset the Soviet Union and eventually win the gold medal.

- *Realize No One Knows*: In his column "Graduates, Are You Ready for the Most Important Secret in the Whole Wide World?" *Wall Street Journalist* Jason Gay wrote:

> Nobody really knows what they're doing. Life is a series of leaps and educated guesses. Sometimes, uneducated guesses. We can practice, prepare, and read all the instruction manuals, but we're really all making this up as we go along. Even the people who seem like they know what they're doing—they don't know what they're doing all the time.[10]

[10] Gay, J. 2019. "Graduates, Are You Ready for the Most Important Secret in the Whole Wide World?." *Wall Street Journal*, May 10. https://wsj.com/articles/graduates-are-you-ready-for-the-most-important-secret-in-the-whole-wide-world-11557480629 (accessed May 20, 2019).

If you want to be relevant to the 21st century workplace, help everyone you encounter as much as you can. Since no one really knows what they are doing, any help you might be willing to provide would make you a valuable team member. Also, if you accept that no one knows what they are doing, that means you don't either. So commit to lifelong learning, continue to challenge yourself to grow, and travel outside your comfort zone as much as possible.

- *Feel Deeply*: In the 2006 American comedy-drama road film *Little Miss Sunshine*, Steve Carell's character Frank is a professor and preeminent scholar of Proust. Toward the end of the movie, he tells Paul Dano's character Dwayne

> when Proust gets down to the end of his life, he looks back and he decides that all the years he suffered—those were the best years of his life. Because they made him who he was. They forced him to think and grow, and to feel very deeply.[11]

If you want to remain relevant to the 21st century workplace, feel deeply. Travel outside of your comfort zone. Take on new challenges. Attempt a job that you think might be out of your skill set. Grow. Think. Feel. Doing so just might help you be that person that others want to work alongside.

The humanities will remain relevant to the 21st century workplace if higher education institutions address the disconnects outlined in this publication. Additionally, now that humanities majors know the disconnects, they can leverage their own self-reliance and search for answers as they travel down the path to relevance in the 21st century.

---

[11] *Little Miss Sunshine* script, https://scriptslug.com/script/little-miss-sunshine-2006, (accessed May 20, 2019).

Recent Humanities Publications

Despite the declining number of humanities majors, or perhaps because of, there are a variety of new and vibrant resources available to help people understand the value of the humanities. Most notably is the free online resource Study the Humanities Toolkit as well as the following list of recent publications:

- George Anders, *You Can Do Anything: The Surprising Power of a "Useless" Liberal Arts Education,* Little, Brown, and Company, 2017.
- Scott Hartley, *The Fuzzy and the Techie: Why the Liberal Arts Will Rule the Digital World,* Houghton Mifflin Harcourt, 2017.
- Christian Madsbjerg, *Sensemaking: The Power of the Humanities in the Age of the Algorithm,* Hachette Books, 2017.
- Gary Saul Morson and Morton Schapiro, *Cents and Sensibility: What Economics Can Learn from the Humanities*, Princeton University Press, 2017.
- Randall Stross, *A Practical Education: Why Liberal Arts Majors Make Great Employees,* Stanford University Press, 2017.
- Fareed Zaharia, *In Defense of a Liberal Education* Kastella Rylestone, LLC, 2015.

The Study the Humanities Toolkit

The Study the Humanities Toolkit located at www.studythehumanities.org is a collection of resources for higher education faculty and administrators to use in making the case for the value of studying the humanities as an undergraduate. The site contains six sections of free information divided across a variety of issues: performance, skills, careers, examples, benefits, and articles.

- *Performance*: Based on available data on learning outcomes and performance for those who major in the humanities, this section presents an empirical case that humanities majors develop critical thinking and reasoning skills.
- *Skills*: This section presents the findings of a series of surveys conducted by the Association of American Colleges and Universities (AAC&U) that show employers are looking for recent graduates who have the skills that humanities majors develop through their studies.
- *Careers*: Humanities majors find lucrative careers. This section draws on employment and salary data to make the case that humanities majors find lucrative careers in a variety of fields.
- *Benefits*: This section makes the case that the benefits of majoring in the humanities are lifelong and extend beyond the marketplace.
- *Articles*: Taken from a wide variety of publications, the articles in this section make the case for studying the humanities and employ a variety of different arguments to do so.

Anders, G. 2017. *You Can Do Anything: The Surprising Power of a "Useless" Liberal Arts Education,* Little Brown and Company.

An easy to read publication, and the most practical among the list here, designed to provide relief to liberal arts majors that they can indeed have a wide variety of careers. English majors can work in sales. Anthropology majors can leverage their skills and work in market research. Classics majors can have a career in management consulting and philosophy majors can find employment in investing. "At any stage of your career, you can bring a humanist's grace to our rapidly evolving high-tech future. And if you know how to attack the job market, your opportunities will be vast."

Hartley, S. 2017. *The Fuzzy and the Techie: Why the Liberal Arts Will Rule the Digital World,* Houghton Mifflin Harcourt.

Hartley believes that fuzzies (humanities majors) are playing the key roles in developing the most creative and successful new business ideas and not the techies (computer science majors). Humanities majors better understand the life issues that need solving and offer the best approaches for doing so. By examining the fuzzy-techie collaborations that are disrupting today's world, Hartley demonstrates that the liberal arts are at the center of innovation in business, education, and government, and, thus, are still relevant today. Liberal arts majors bring context to code, ethics to algorithms, and the soft skills so vital to spurring growth.

Madsbjerg, C. 2017. *Sensemaking: The Power of the Humanities in the Age of the Algorithm*, Hachette Books.

The modern obsession with big data often masks stunning deficiencies. Blind devotion to number crunching imperils businesses, schools, and governments. Too many companies have lost touch with the humanity of their customers, while marginalizing workers with liberal arts-based skills. Madsbjerg coined the term *sensemaking* to highlight the value of deep, nuanced engagement with culture, language, and history to help address some of today's most pressing issues that big data alone is unable to solve.

Morson, G.S., and M. Schapiro. 2018. *Cents and Sensibility: What Economics Can Learn from the Humanities*. Princeton University Press.

Morson and Schapiro argue that the study of literature offers economists ways to make their models more realistic, their predictions more accurate, and their policies more effective and just. Demonstrating the relevance of the great writers to the field of economics remains the most esoteric publication in this list. For those looking for a detailed illustration of the value of the humanities, this book remains original, provocative, and inspiring.

Stross, R. 2017. *A Practical Education: Why Liberal Arts Majors Make Great Employees*, Stanford University Press.

Stross provides a practical explanation of the tangible merits of the humanities. *A Practical Education* reminds readers that the most useful training for an unknowable future is the universal, time-tested preparation of a liberal education. *A Practical Education* investigates the real-world experiences of graduates with humanities majors, the majors that would seem the least employable in Silicon Valley's engineering-centric workplaces. When given a first opportunity, these majors thrive in work roles that no one would have predicted.

These resources support J. M. Olejarz's observation in the *Harvard Business Review* that "people are beginning to realize that to effectively tackle today's biggest social and technological challenges, we need to think critically about their human context—something humanities graduates happen to be well trained to do."[1] To illustrate the relevance of the humanities to the 21st century workplace, however, we need to begin with having higher education admit to several problems that continue to exist.

Zaharia, F. 2015. *In Defense of a Liberal Education* Kastella Rylestone, LLC.

Zakaria eloquently expounds on the virtues of a liberal arts education—how to write clearly, how to express yourself convincingly, and how to think analytically. He turns our leaders' vocational argument on its head. American routine manufacturing jobs continue to get automated or outsourced, and specific vocational knowledge is often outdated within a few years. Engineering is a great profession, but key value-added skills you will also need are creativity, lateral thinking, design, communication, storytelling, and, more than anything, the ability to continually learn and enjoy learning—precisely the gifts of a liberal education.

---

[1] Olejarz, J.M. July-August 2017. "Liberal Arts in the Data Age." *Harvard Business Review*, https://hbr.org/2017/07/liberal-arts-in-the-data-age (accessed February 22, 2019).

About the Author

Dr. Michael Edmondson is the Interim Dean, College of Professional Studies and Dean, Professional Education and Lifelong Learning at New Jersey City University. He has published four books with Business Experts Press: *Marketing Your Value: 9 Steps to Navigate Your Career*, *Major in Happiness: Debunking the College Major Fallacies*, *Success: Theory and Practice*, and *Strategic Thinking and Writing*. Dr. Edmondson has a BA from Cabrini University, an MA from Villanova University and a PhD from Temple University.

Index

Ability
to contextualize, 75
to influence peers, 73
Academic programs, 3, 98
Active listening, 74
Acuff, J., 94–95
AdAge, 49
Agility, 62
American Historical Association (AHA), xxv
American Society for Engineering Education (ASEE), 12
Aoun, J., 117
Arithmetic subject, 10
Arts, 7–8
Association of American Colleges and Universities (AAC&U), xxxiv, 4–5, 11–12, 24, 33, 34, 103
Astronomy subject, 10

Belief, 113
Bérubé, M., 16
Best v. Right, 123–124
Booth, W. C., 2
Botelho, E., 32
Botstein, L., 120, xxviii
Brookings Institution, 80
Brown, H. J., 95
Business executive pedigree, 32–34

CareerBuilder survey (2018), 58
Career development, xv, 41, 68
Career path, 97
Carly Fiorina, History major from Stanford University, 29
Carol Browner, an English major from University of Florida, 28
Casnocha, B., 115
Catch-22 (Heller), 96
The CEO Next Door: Based on a Breakthrough Study of over 2,600 Leaders (Botelho and Powell), 32
Chesteron, A., 94
Chief executive officer (CEO), 26–31
Christensen, C., xxx
Chronicle of Higher Education (Surber), 16
The Chronicle of Higher Education (Stover), 3, 25
Chrucky, A., 13, 14
College majors, 31, 33, 35, 69, 83–84, 98, 112
The College of Idaho's 2010-11 Catalog, 3
Colvin, G., 44, 80–81, 91
Connor, W. R., 15
Coolidge, C., 92
Courage, 75
Craig, R., xxxiii, 23, 84
Creation, 47–48
Cronon, W., 7
"C-Suite Challenge," 36
Cuban, M., 35–36
Curiosity and positivity, 74
Currey, M., 95

Daily Rituals: How Artists Work (Currey), 95
Daniels, M., xxxiii, 23–24
David and Goliath: Underdogs, Misfits, and The Art of Battling Giants (Gladwell), 124
Davidson, C. N., 117, xxxii
Deci, E. L., 101, 110
Decision making process, 9, 56, 71, 74, 112–114
Decoding the Cost of College: The Case for Transparent Financial Aid Award Letters, 123
Dell'Antonia, K. J., 122

Deming, D., 41
Dialectic subject, 9
Didion, J., 108
Disconnect, 2–7, 22–26, 42–45, 63–67, 85–88, 102–105
Division for Sustainable Development Goals (DSDG), 69–70
Donald. R. Knauss, a history major from Indiana University, 29–30
Donna Dubinsky, History major from Yale University, 28
Duckworth, A., 91

Ebner, K., xxxii
Educare, 8
Education among the Liberal Arts (Horn), 13–14
Eleutheros, 7
Ely Callaway, History major from Emory University, 28
Emotional intelligence, 74
Empathy, 73
Emsi, 43, 44
Engineering and A Liberal Education (Grasso), 12
Eric, G., 6
Etymology, 7–9
Experience, 46
Expert, 47

Facebook, 90
Fitch ratings, xxix
Flexiblity, 113
Florence Steinberg, a history major from University of Massachusetts, Amherst, 30–31
Focus, 48, 113
Forbes, xxvii, xxxiii, 23
Franklin, B., 92
Free, 8
Freedman, J. O., 14
Fried, J., 95
Friedman, T., 42
The Future of Work: Attract New Talent, Build Better Leaders, and Create a Competitive Organization (Morgan), 116–117

Gallup-Lumina Foundation (2014), xxxiii, 22
Gallup-Purdue University Survey, 66
Gallup-Sharecare Well-Being Index, 105, 106
Gay, J., 124
Gelatt, C., 112
Gelatt, H. B., 112
Geometry subject, 10
Gilliland, M. W., 8
Gladwell, M., 124
Glaser, A., 103
Grade point average (GPA), 33, 65, 112
Grammar subject, 9
Grasso, D., 12
Greenwald, R. A., 79
Grit: The Power of Passion and Perseverance (Duckworth), 91–93

Haefner, R., 37
Hansson, D. H., 95
Harvard University, 14
Heller, J., 96
Herb Scannell, an English major from Boston College, 30
Hersh, R., 6
Higher education, 17, 22, 26, 43
Higher education institutions, xxix–xxxi, 4, 21, 23, 24, 40, 42, 44–45, 59, 66, 77–81, 99, 101–103, 105, 115, 121
Hoffman, R., 115
Horn, F., 13–14
Humanities, 7
  departments, 63
  graduates, 33–34, 36, 40, 49, 77, 89, 108
  liberal arts and, 26
  majors, 26, 27, 34–35, 42–45, 50, 57–59, 61–63, 65–69, 71–77, 91–97
Humans Are Underrated: What High Achievers Know that

Brilliant Machines Never Will (Colvin), 44, 80–81
Humility, 74
Humphreys, D., 33, 103
Hutton, T. S., 17

Institute for College Access and Success, 62
Internships, 88–90
Irzik, G., 8
Issue-based career path, 69–72
Ives, C., 96

Jaschik, S., 4
Jeffrey R. Immelt, a math major from Dartmouth College, 29
Jill Barad, an English major from Queens College, New York City, 27
Job, 77–79
  requirements, 76–77
John J. Mack, a history major from Duke University, 30

Kak, S., xxx
Kaplan, R. S., 115–116
Kathleen, H., 9
Kathryn Fuller, an English major from Brown University, 29
Kelly, P., 33
Kenneth Chenault, History major from Bowdoin College, 28
Kierkegaard, S., 122
Kimberly Kelleher, a history major from University of Wisconsin, Madison, 29
Knowledge career path, 67–69
Kristof, N., 39

Labor Department, 93–94
Leadership, 46, 73–75
Leisure, 122–123
Liberal, 7
Liberal arts, 2–8
  colleges, 17–18
  vs. liberal education, 11–15
Liberal education and political liberalism, 15–16
Lifelong learning, 115–117
LifeTwist study, 93–94, 97
Little Miss Sunshine, 125

McAvoy, W., xxxii, 22
Major in Happiness: Debunking the College Major Fallacies (Edmondson), 71–72
Managerial positions, 73–75
Mandel, M. S., 17–18
Marketing Your Value: 9 Steps to Navigate Your Career (Edmondson), 42
Marketplace, 25
Markus, H. R., 108–109
Mezirow, J., 104
Michael Eisner, English major from Denison University, 28–29
Michael Lynne, an English major from Brooklyn College, 30
Modern Language Association (MLA), xxv
Moody, J., xxix
Morgan, J., 116–117
Motivation, 47
Music subject, 10

Narrative Economics (Shiller), 119
National Association of Colleges and Employers (NACE), 35, 88, 90, 104
National Center for Education Statistics, 19
The National Leadership Council, 37
The National Science Foundation, 77
The New Education: How to Revolutionize the University to Prepare Students for a World in Flux (Davidson), 117
The Newsroom (television series), xxxii, 22
The New York Times, 39, 41, 122
Nola, R., 8
Nussbaum, M., 13

Observation skills, 74
O'Neill, N., 88–89

Optimism, 113
Oral and written communication skills, 74

Pascarella, E., 2
Pasquerella, L., xxxiv, 24
Passion, 46–47
Passivists, 97
Perception disconnect, 63–65
Personal development, 116
Personal statement, 54–57
PhD certification, 63–64
Pickus, N., xxxii
Pinker, S., 102
Political liberalism, liberal education and, 15–16
Possible Selves (Markus), 108–109
Powell, K., 32
Problem-solving, 74, 85
Professional development, 66, 75, 103, 116

Quadrivium, 10
Quitter: Closing the Gap Between Your Day Job and Your Dream Job (Acuff), 94–95

Reinventionsists, 97
Relationship building, 75
The Relevance of the Humanities to the 21st Century Workplace, xxxiv
Resilience, 74
Responsibility, 76
Return on investment (ROI), xxvii
Return-on-investment (ROI), 61
Rhetoric subject, 10
Robot-Proof: Higher Education in the Age of Artificial Intelligence (Aoun), 117
Rosenberg, B. C., xxv
Rubenstein, D. M., 27
Ryan, R., 101
Ryan, R. M., 110

Samuel J. Palmisano, History major from Johns Hopkins University, 30
Saving the Liberal Arts (Schneider and Sigelman), 120–121, xxix
Schneider, M., 120–121, xxix
Schultz. H., 21–22
Scorziello, S., 75–76
Self-awareness, 75, 104
Self-determination, 108–112
Self-determination theory (SDT), 101, 110
Self-reliance, 122
Shellenbarger, S., 96
Shiller, R., 119
Shoenberg, R., 11, 12
Sigelman, M., 120–121, xxix
Skill, 34–38, 46
Skill-based career path, 72–77
Skin in the Game: Hidden Asymmetries in Daily Life (Taleb), 87–88
Slogans, 49–50
Slouching Towards Bethlehem (Didion), 108
Specializeation, 45–46
TheStart-up of You: Adapt to the Future, Invest in Yourself, and Transform Your Career (Hoffman and Casnocha), 115
Stover, J., 3
Strassburger, J., 5
Strategy, 48
Strauss, L., 13, 14
The Study the Humanities Toolkit, 127–130
Subjects, 9–11
Subtle maneuvers, 94–98
Success, xxv–xxvi
Success factors, 52–54
Successful people, 109–110
Surber, J. P., 16
Sustainable Development Goals (SDGs), 69–71
Swarthmore College, 14–15

Talbert, R., 12
Taleb, N. N., 87–88
Talent Is Overrated: What Really Separates World-Class

Performers from Everyone Else (Colvin), 91
Teaching job, 79
Tim Donahue, English major from John Carroll University, 28
Traditionalists, 97
Trivium, 9–10

Uncertainty, 112–115
Undergraduate education, xv, 3, 18, 23, 31, 33, 34, 42–44, 67, 69, 72, 77, 80, 98, 105, 127
United Nations Department of Economic and Social Affairs (UNDESA), 69–70
The University in a Corporate Culture (Eric), 6
University of Toronto, 96–97
USA Today (Scorziello), 75–76
Utica College, 17

Value proposition, 49–52
Veitch, J., 17
Vocational knowledge, 97
Volatile, uncertain, complex, and ambiguous (VUCA), xxxi, 1, 23, 24, 44, 85, 105, 112, 117

Wadhwani, E., xxix
Wadhwa, V., 13, 39–40
The Wall Street Journal, xxviii, 33, 96, 120
Washington, D., 92
Well-being, 105–108
What's LIBERAL about the Liberal Arts? (Bérubé), 16
What We Don't Know about the Effects of Liberal Arts Education (Pascarella), 2–3
Williams, R. A., 3
Willingness, 75
Workfolio, 57–58

Zakaria, F., xxvi

OTHER TITLES IN THE HUMAN RESOURCE MANAGEMENT AND ORGANIZATIONAL BEHAVIOR COLLECTION

- *The Generation Myth* by Michael J. Urick
- *Practicing Leadership* by Alan S. Gutterman
- *Practicing Management* by Alan S. Gutterman
- *Women Leaders* by Sapna Welsh and Caroline Kersten
- *Comparative Management Studies* by Nelson E. Brestoff
- *Cross-Cultural Leadership Studies* by Richard M. Contino

Announcing the Business Expert Press Digital Library

Concise e-books business students need for classroom and research

This book can also be purchased in an e-book collection by your library as

- a one-time purchase,
- that is owned forever,
- allows for simultaneous readers,
- has no restrictions on printing, and
- can be downloaded as PDFs from within the library community.

Our digital library collections are a great solution to beat the rising cost of textbooks. E-books can be loaded into their course management systems or onto students' e-book readers.
The **Business Expert Press** digital libraries are very affordable, with no obligation to buy in future years. For more information, please visit **www.businessexpertpress.com/librarians**. To set up a trial in the United States, please email **sales@businessexpertpress.com.**

CPSIA information can be obtained
at www.ICGtesting.com
Printed in the USA
JSHW020826190520
5759JS00006B/129